I0167881

Orthodox Christian
Bible Commentary

COLOSSIANS
1 THESSALONIANS
2 THESSALONIANS

By His Grace Bishop Youssef

ST Mary & Moses ABBEY PRESS

Orthodox Christian Bible Commentary: Colossians, 1 Thessalonians, 2 Thessalonians

Designed & Published by:
St. Mary & St. Moses Abbey Press
101 S. Vista Dr., Sandia, TX 78383
stmabbeypress.com

Printed in the United States of America

Cover design image photo by Katherine Nawar,
and icon from Bedour Latif and Youssef Nassief.

Library of Congress Control Number: 2014934844

✠

❧ *Contents* ❧

St. Paul's Epistle to the

Colossians

AUTHOR: St. Paul. The author of this letter is St. Paul, as it is clear from the first verse, which reads: "Paul, an apostle of Jesus Christ by the will of God." Also in 4:18, St. Paul concludes the epistle by telling its recipients: "This salutation by my own hand— Paul." All the Church Fathers confirm that St. Paul is the author of this letter.

PLACE & TIME: St. Paul wrote this letter to Colossians while he was imprisoned in Rome, between 61 and 63 AD (Col. 4:18). Thus, this epistle is grouped among three other prison epistles (Ephesians, Philippians, and Philemon) written during that period of time while he was in prison.

THE COLOSSIANS - RECIPIENTS OF THIS LETTER

The recipients of this letter were the Colossians—the church at Colosse. Colosse in modern times is situated in Turkey. With nearby Laodicea and Hierapolis, it was part of a triad of cities nearby to each other in what is known as the Lycos valley. Colosse had both pagans and Jews mingling together, which posed a big challenge for the believers who faced the imposition of Jewish and pagan beliefs on their new Christian faith. One of the major heresies of the time is called Gnosticism. That word means, "growing in knowledge." Gnostics used to teach that sin results from a lack of knowledge. They also taught that physical material is a sin. For that reason, they had a very difficult time comprehending the notion that God took flesh, which flesh is understood by the Gnostics to be sinful. In advancement of their views on the sinfulness of all that is material or physical, they proposed the belief that God did not create physical material, but rather certain powers which emanated from God (called Aeons) existed and eventually the creation of the material world came about without the direct doing of God. Hence, it was believed that God did not create the physical world, but merely did so by means of some other powers emanating from Him. To resolve the flaw of physical existence and the material world, they believed in a savior, Aeon—Christ—who was to help humanity to achieve true knowledge (i.e., Gnosis). They believed in Christ as being an Aeon, emanating from the fullness of God, but not the same as God in His full capacity. They taught that it is not proper to worship God directly. In order to be humble, they must only worship the mediating powers—the Aeons. For example, they would worship angels as well as Christ because both were mediators. Since they believed that physical material was sinful, they would engage in harsh asceticism to discipline the flesh, believing that if they put to death the flesh through such discipline, then a person can increase in knowledge and connection with God. Gnostics wanted to impose their beliefs on Christians, and this is one of the reasons St. Paul wrote his letter to the Colossians and dealt with such false beliefs and heresies.

Who preached the gospel to Colosse?
We learn from the first chapter in verses 5-8 that Epaphras (who was a Colossian himself—Col. 4:12) was the one who preached the Gospel to the Colossians. He is known to have also preached in the two other cities nearby, Hierapolis and Laodicea. Epaphras was like a disciple of St. Paul, often sending reports to St. Paul about various matters.

Philemon and his family
A well-known family in the city of Colosse was that of Philemon, his wife Apphia, and their son Archippus. The church at Colosse used to meet at their house (Col. 4:17 and Philem. 1-2). Philemon's servant Onesimus, after fleeing and meeting with St. Paul, returned to become a Christian and member of the church at Colosse.

PURPOSE FOR WRITING THIS LETTER

St. Paul received a report from Epaphras (Col. 1:7-8, 2:5). While it was a very positive letter, there were a number of dangers which were exhibited.

- Apostasy—relapsing to paganism (Col. 1:21-23, 2:6, 3:5-11).

- Pagan and Jewish Beliefs: philosophies of men (Col. 2:8), Judaistic ceremonialism (2:11, 16-17), angel worship (2:18), and harsh asceticism (2:20-23).

The purpose of this letter was to warn the Colossians against apostasy (relapse) and also to make it clear that in Christ—we find our satisfaction. He is all-sufficient. He also proved the divinity of Christ—He is God in the flesh. He made it clear that the only knowledge is the knowledge of Christ, through whom we can be saved and acquire our eternal salvation and inheritance.

THEME

Christ, the fullness of God, the pre-eminent, and all-sufficient Savior (Col. 2:9-10).

Similarity between Colossians and Ephesians

If you compare this letter with the letter to the Ephesians, you will notice much similarity. Actually many ideas and verses are exactly the same in both letters. It is interesting to notice that in the letter to the Colossians, St. Paul focused on Christ as the head of the Church; while in his letter to the Ephesians, he spoke about the Church, the body of Christ.

OUTLINE OF COLOSSIANS

Chapter 1
• Salutation (1-2)
• Thanksgiving and prayer (3-14)
• Preeminence of Christ in creation (15-17)
• Preeminence of Christ in the Church (18-23)
• St. Paul's ministry (24-29)

Chapter 2
• St. Paul's concern for their salvation (1-7)
• Against false theology (8-15)
• Against false spirituality (16-23)

Chapter 3
• New life with Christ (1-4)
• Putting off the old man (5-11)
• Putting off the new man (12-17)
• Life application (18-25)

Chapter 4
• Instructions to masters (1)
• Prayers (2-4)
• Proper conduct (5-6)
• Greetings (7-14)
• Concluding remarks (15-18)

1

1:1 Paul, an apostle of Jesus Christ by the will of God. He started this chapter by identifying himself as the *"apostle of Jesus Christ by the will of God."* He uses this title in order to relay the notion that this letter is authoritative. He is writing to them with the authority that he received from God, as an apostle according to the will of God. Thus, the teachings of this letter are not simply in accordance with his own mind, but as a good steward, he is exhorting them on how to conduct their lives in a godly way. ✠ When he writes that he is an *"apostle ... by the will of God,"* he is indicating that any ministry, especially that of the priesthood, is a calling from God. *"No man takes this honor to himself, but he who is called by God, just as Aaron was"* (Heb. 5:4).

and Timothy our brother. St. Timothy was accompanying him at the time this letter was written. Although Timothy was his son in faith and also his disciple, yet we can see exhibited the humility of St. Paul in addressing St. Timothy as his brother in the faith and in the ministry (both of them being bishops).

1:2 To the saints. He uses the word *"saints"* to remind them of their status in Christ. We are called to be saints, to be holy and perfect, conducting our lives in a godly way.

and faithful brethren in Christ who are in Colosse. St. Paul calls them *"brethren"* because all of us are children of God. In this sense, we are all brethren in the body of Christ, in the Church, in Christ Jesus, because the Church is the body of Christ.

Grace to you and peace. Here we have St. Paul's benediction to the Colossians. Grace and peace are the most needed gifts for all of us, because without the grace of God, we cannot achieve anything. The grace of God is the power that helps us in our lives. He is praying that the grace and peace of God accompanies them in the midst of all the hardships and afflictions of the world.

from God our Father and the Lord Jesus Christ. St. Paul emphasizes the divinity of our Lord Jesus Christ. Grace and peace come from God the Father and the Lord Jesus Christ. He is relaying in this statement the notion of equality between God the Father and Jesus Christ.

1:3 **We give thanks to the God and Father of our Lord Jesus Christ, praying always for you.** In the following verses (3-14), St. Paul gives thanks to God on behalf of the Colossians. He received a report about them from Epaphras and was very happy when he read the report. This is because their faith and love (including their works) were growing. The good report of the flock usually makes the heart of the servant rejoice and causes the servant to give thanks to God on their behalf, even in the midst of hardships. Although St. Paul was in prison at the time he wrote this letter, he was exceedingly happy to hear about the progress of the Colossians, which stirred his heart to give thanks to God and pray for them.

1:4 **since we heard.** In his use of the word *"heard,"* we understand this to mean that St. Paul is not the one who established the church in Colosse. Rather, he heard from Epaphras about the believers there.

of your faith in Christ Jesus and of your love for all the saints. Among the things St. Paul learned about this city, is that a number of people accepted the faith, and the faith they retained

was made manifest in good works. "Love," as we read about it in the Holy Scriptures, is not simply an emotion, but involves works (see 1 Cor. 13 where "love" is expressed as a series of things you do, not just an emotion you feel).

1:5 **because of the hope which is laid up for you in heaven.** St. Paul also gives thanks for the *"hope which is laid up"* for the Colossians "in heaven." What is this hope? It is the hope of salvation, inheritance, and living eternally with God. St. Paul is telling them that he is thankful for their hope in heaven, that they will inherit the kingdom of God about which they learned by the preaching of the gospel by Epaphras. They are no longer foreigners, aliens, and strangers, but now they are citizens of heaven who are endowed with an inheritance there.

of which you heard before in the word of the truth of the gospel. By this we can learn that the only true knowledge is the knowledge of the word of God. The philosophies of men, which were a major interference in the faith of the Colossians, are not truth, as opposed to those things which come from the gospel of Christ.

1:6 **which has come to you, as it has also in all the world, and is bringing forth fruit.** This gospel has been preached not only to the Colossians but throughout the world. Thus, the truth of the gospel is not for a certain race, nation, tribe, or tongue. Rather, it is for the whole world. When we accept this truth in our hearts, it will definitely bring forth fruit (see Gal. 5:22 for the fruit of the Spirit, including "love," which the Colossians had been exhibiting abundantly [cf., Col. 1:4, 8]).

as it is also among you since the day you heard and knew the grace of God in truth. It is interesting to note that *"since the day"* the Colossians accepted Christ, they immediately began to bear fruit in their new Christian lives. In other words, they were doers of the word, not just hearers (cf., James 1:22).

1:7-8   as you also learned from Epaphras, our dear fellow servant ... who also declared to us your love in the Spirit. Epaphras is being described as a servant of Christ. Referring to him as a "dear fellow servant" shows us the love between the apostles and their disciples. We, as servants, should have this love toward one another. It is very sad when we see servants, deacons, or church board members not loving one another. They have to bear the fruit of love if they are disciples of Christ. *"By this all will know that you are My disciples, if you have love for one another"* (John 13:35).

who is a faithful minister of Christ on your behalf. All of us serve Christ, but God appoints people in different capacities to do different things. Epaphras was appointed by God to preach to the Colossians.

1:9   For this reason we also, since the day we heard it, do not cease to pray for you. St. Paul heard of the good report of Epaphras about the Colossians and was joyful upon hearing it. From this joy sprung forth thanksgiving and also prayer. His prayer, as you will read, reflects a yearning that they continue as they started, abounding in the fruit of the Spirit.

do not cease to pray for you and to ask. Servants (whether they be clergy or laymen) should never stop praying for those whom they serve. The great servant and prophet of Israel, Samuel, said, *"Far be it from me that I should sin against the LORD in ceasing to pray for you"* (1 Samuel 12:23). What follows is the substance of St. Paul's prayer for the Colossians.

that you may be filled with the knowledge of His will. The starting point in the life of any Christian is to know the will of God. It is not just any knowledge that we should seek, but more specifically, the *"knowledge of His will."* When you *"know the truth ... the truth shall make you free"* (John 8:32). That is why St. Paul prays for them for the knowledge of God's will.

in all wisdom and spiritual understanding. How can we learn the will of God? We should study the Holy Scriptures because it reveals to us the mind of Christ and the will of God. We are not to simply seek a superficial knowledge. Many of us know some stories from the Bible, some stories about the saints, but how many people have deep spiritual understanding that fills their heart and mind and allows them to understand the will of God? This knowledge should be *"in all wisdom,"* knowing the basic principles of the word of God. *"Spiritual understanding"* is the skill of applying the principles—the wisdom ascertained about God. Thus, the knowledge of God's will comes from learning the basic principles of His word (in all wisdom) and applying it (with spiritual understanding).

1:10 **that you may walk worthy of the Lord, fully pleasing Him.** The purpose of acquiring an understanding of the will of God is to *"walk worthy of the Lord."* When we do this, we will be pleasing to God. How can a person *"walk worthy of the Lord"* without knowing Him? Imagine, for example, you are working for a company: you need to know the regulations and policies of this company in order to please your boss; but without knowing his or her will, then it will be difficult to appease the

leaders of your organization. Similarly, St. Paul teaches us that first we must be filled with the knowledge of God's will, and that should turn into action.

fully pleasing Him. Notice that St. Paul does not simply say *"pleasing"* God, but *"fully"* pleasing Him. It is not enough to partially please Him, but to seek to *"fully"* delight God in us. *"'But let him who glories glory in this, that he understands and knows Me, that I am the LORD, exercising lovingkindness, judgment, and righteousness in the earth. For in these I delight,' says the LORD"* (Jer. 9:24).

being fruitful in every good work. We need to bear the fruit of the Spirit in our lives (Gal. 5:22). As the Lord said, *"Every tree that does not bear good fruit is cut down and thrown into the fire"* (Matt. 7:19). He also tells us, *"You did not choose Me, but I chose you and appointed you that you should go and bear fruit, and that your fruit should remain, that whatever you ask the Father in My name He may give you"* (John 15:16).

and increasing in the knowledge of God. When we know the will of God and walk worthy of the Lord, this will lead to the knowledge of God Himself. St. Paul uses the word *"increasing"* because knowing God is a lifelong experience, not only on earth but also in heaven: *"And this is eternal life, that they may know You, the only true God, and Jesus Christ whom You have sent"* (John 17:3). Because God is infinite, then to know God, we need infinite time. Even during our eternal life, we will increase in the knowledge of God. Thus, no one can claim they know everything about God.

1:11 strengthened with all might, according to His glorious power. When we increase in the knowledge of God, we will be strengthened by God's glorious power. St. Paul is not speaking of simply intellectual knowledge, but about experiential knowledge. When we experience God in our lives, this experience will strengthen us. This strength is not according to our human capabilities, but rather with God's *"might"* and *"glorious power."*

for all patience and longsuffering with joy. We need to be strong because in our spiritual journey, we will face many hardships and afflictions. To endure such tribulation, we need not only patience and longsuffering, but also the spirit of joy, lest we become depressed from all the hardships and sufferings. Thus, by growing in the knowledge of God through our experiences with Him, we will gain patience and longsuffering, and while in the midst of difficulties, we will be able to sustain our joy. St. Paul, although he was in prison, rejoiced.

1:12 giving thanks to the Father. Out of joy, we should give thanks. Thanksgiving is not words, but rather an attitude of gratefulness. Being filled with the knowledge of God, walking worthy of the Lord, pleasing Him, we will be strengthened with His glorious power in all patience and longsuffering with joy. All of this should translate into thanksgiving to the Father. St. Paul gives several reasons for giving thanks to God:

who has qualified us to be partakers of the inheritance of the saints in the light. We were previously not qualified to be partakers of eternal life. Children are those who are eligible to receive an inheritance from their father. *"The Spirit Himself bears witness with our spirit that we are children of God, and if children, then heirs—heirs of God and joint heirs with Christ"* (Rom. 8:16-17). By nature, we are servants, not children, and thus, would not normally be qualified for the Father's inheritance. But God qualified us to be partakers of the inheritance, sending His Son as our Bridegroom, and then, we became united to the Bridegroom because we—the Church—are His bride. Through this marriage, we become children of the Father and joint heirs of His kingdom. *"'For this reason a man shall leave his father and mother and be joined to his wife, and the two shall become one flesh.' This is a great mystery, but I speak concerning Christ and the church"* (Eph. 5:31-32). This is the manner we received *"adoption as sons by Jesus Christ to Himself, according to the pleasure of His will"* (Eph. 1:5; see also Rom. 8:15, 23, 9:4; Gal. 4:5). This is the manner by which we become "qualified" and are able *"to be partakers of the inheritance of the saints in the light."*

in the light. Christ is the light of the world, as we say in the Creed, *"Light of Light."*

1:13 **He has delivered us from the power of darkness and conveyed us into the kingdom of the Son of His love.** St. Paul compares between the kingdom of Satan—which is darkness—and the kingdom of God— which is light. Before we became qualified to the inheritance of the light, we were sitting in darkness: Speaking of Christ's coming, St. Matthew writes, *"The people who sat in darkness have seen a great light, and upon those who sat in the region and shadow of death light has dawned"* (Matt. 4:16). Satan is the prince of the world, and we were previously living in his kingdom. But Christ came, and not only delivered us from the power of darkness, but He also took the further step of conveying us (transferring us) into His kingdom of light.

the kingdom of the Son. St. Paul describes Christ as a King here. Notice that St. Paul uses the past tense here—*"conveyed."* That is because the kingdom of the Son started on the day of His crucifixion. That is the beginning of the "Millennial Reign" (which is not a literal thousand years), of which

is spoken in the Book of Revelation and often misinterpreted. We are not waiting for the Second Coming of Christ in order for Him to initiate the Millennial Reign. He already has come and is reigning as King. That is why you hear in the Divine Liturgy that we call Christ our Lord, God, Savior, and King of us all. Now, we are living in the *"kingdom of the Son of His love."*

Son of His love. God is love, therefore the Son of God is the Son of His love.

1:14 **in whom we have redemption through His blood, the forgiveness of sins.** Here St. Paul answers the question which arises out of the two previous verses. How did all of this happen, that we were made *"qualified to the inheritance of the saints in the light, being delivered from the power of darkness and conveyed into the kingdom of the Son of His love?"* All of this happened through the blood of our Lord Jesus Christ. When He shed His precious blood on the cross, He redeemed us (i.e., delivered us from the power of Satan) and forgave our sins. Now, we are saved and qualified to be partakers of the inheritance of the saints.

1:15-17 St. Paul starts to speak about Christ specifically. As explained in the introduction, Gnosticism—an increasingly popular belief system at the time—taught that Christ was not God, but was simply one of the emanations from God (one of the many powers, or Aeons, which proceeded from God, but was not equal to the source from whom they came—not being equal to God). That is why St. Paul wanted to emphasize that Christ is God in the flesh, the second hypostasis of the Holy Trinity, who came and took flesh in order to redeem us. Before speaking about His preeminence in the Church as its head, St. Paul focuses here on Christ's preeminence in regards to all creation prior to His incarnation. God is eternal, and Christ, being God, is eternal.

He is the image of the invisible God. *"The invisible God"* refers to the hypostasis of the Father. No one has seen the Father at any time, but Christ revealed Him to us. *"No one has seen God at any time. The only begotten Son, who is in the bosom of the Father, He has declared Him"* (John 1:18). Christ is the *"image,"* meaning that He is of the same essence of the Father. He is light of light, and true God of true God. Think of this: I cannot see your spirit, but I see your body. In a way, we can compare this with the Father (like our spirit), whom we do not see, but Christ, who is the visible expression of His invisible essence. God is invisible, but we can see the Father in the Son, as the Lord said to Philip, *"He who has seen Me has seen the Father"* (John 6:46). Christ is, therefore, the image—that is, of the same essence—of the invisible

God. Christ, *"being the brightness of His glory and the express image of His [i.e., the Father's] person, and upholding all things by the word of His power, when He had by Himself purged our sins, sat down at the right hand of the Majesty on high"* (Heb. 1:3).

the firstborn over all creation. Notice here that St. Paul refers to Christ as the firstborn, not the first-created. Firstborn does not mean that Christ was created. The original Greek word is πρωτότοκος (prototokos), meaning the origin of all creation.

1:16-17   St. Paul gives three reasons for why Christ is regarded as the "firstborn of creation" (v.15): (1) By Him, through Him, and for Him, all things were created. (2) He is before all things. (3) In Him, all things exist.

1:16 For by Him all things were created ... All things were created through Him and for Him. (1) of 3. By Him, through Him, and for Him, all things were created. By Him: Christ is the creator; through Him: God created the word by His Logos, the Word of God, the Lord Jesus Christ (see also John 1:1 and Heb. 1:2); for Him: we are created for His own glory, to fulfill His economy (like a manager who has employees seeking to execute his will). We are for Him, and not the opposite;

many times we want God to comport with our plans, but that is not correct.

that are in heaven and that are on earth, visible and invisible, whether thrones or dominions or principalities or powers. St. Paul is here making clear that Christ is superior than all created beings, including angels (whose various ranks are mentioned here in this verse: thrones, dominions, principalities, powers). In Gnosticism, angels are an emanation from God, just like Christ. However, St. Paul refutes such a belief by clarifying that Christ is the creator of the angels and all visible and invisible things, whether in heaven of on earth.

1:17 **And He is before all things.** (2) of 3. Christ is eternal. Before any creation, including the angels, Christ existed, because He is God and has no beginning and no end. *"In the beginning was the Word, and the Word was with God, and the Word was God. He was in the beginning with God"* (John 1:1-2); Jesus Christ is the same yesterday, today, and forever" (Heb. 13:8).

and in Him all things consist. This means that Christ holds everything together. Who holds all the cosmos? It is the Son, through His wisdom. He is the Pantocrator (a Greek term whose meaning reflects God as Ruler of All, or All-powerful, or Sustainer of the World. It is a noun, whereas the term

that is often used to replace this word—Almighty—is an adjective).

1:18-23 St. Paul moves from discussing the preeminence of Christ in creation to describing the preeminence of Christ in the Church.

1:18 **And He is the head of the body, the church.** As Christ is the firstborn of all creation, with regard to the Church, He is its head through His resurrection when He abolished death by his death. As the world derives its continuity from the Son, the Church also takes her origin, continuity, and life from Christ.

who is the beginning, the firstborn from the dead. Again, St. Paul uses the word "firstborn" to indicate that Christ is the firstborn of those who will live eternally with God. Some may ask, "Well, Lazarus was raised from the dead before Christ, so why is He (Christ) called the firstborn from the dead?" There are two reasons for this: (1) Christ rose from the dead and He did not die again; (2) He rose with a glorified body, the body of the resurrection.

that in all things He may have the preeminence. As the Son has the preeminence in the creation, so too, He also has preeminence in the Church.

No one can say that he or she is higher than Christ, at the minimum for the following reasons: He is the Son of God in the flesh, He is the only one who arose from the dead with a glorified body and never died again, and He is the head of the body by His resurrection.

1:19 **For it pleased the Father that in Him all the fullness should dwell.** The fact that the Son became man and took flesh pleased the Father. In Christ, the fullness of divinity dwells in Him permanently. Note that the word *"dwell"* as understood from the original Greek text of this epistle indicates permanent dwelling, and not just something that could be construed as temporary. God took our nature and made it one with the fullness of His divinity. Since all the fullness of divinity dwells in Christ, then, He can adequately serve in a sense as a point of distribution (*"And of His fullness we have all received, and grace for grace"*—John 1:16); thus, all gifts are distributed from the Son.

1:20 **and by Him to reconcile all things to Himself, by Him, whether things on earth or things in heaven, having made peace through the blood of His cross.** It pleased the Father to let the fullness of divinity dwell in Christ, and also that we would be reconciled to the Father by Christ

through the shedding of His blood on the cross. We were alienated previously from the Father when humanity fell by the sin of Adam and Eve, but Christ reconciled us again with the Father. In this way, God made peace between us and Him, between heaven and earth, man and his brother, and man and himself.

1:21 **And you, who once were alienated and enemies in your mind by wicked works, yet now He has reconciled.** St. Paul tells the recipients of this letter that their church is an illustration of the peace between us and God. The Colossians were once Gentiles, previously considered not to be amongst God's chosen people in the Old Testament. In a way, they were alienated and were enemies in mind (not knowing the will of God—not having the mind of Christ) and in works (not behaving in the manner which the knowledge of God's commandments would require). Now, they have been reconciled to God by being members of the Church, members of His body.

1:22 **in the body of His flesh.** St. Paul emphasizes the true incarnation of Christ, taking an actual *"body"* of *"flesh."* By taking our nature, He sanctified the material, which would combat the Gnostic belief that physical material is evil or sinful.

through death, to present you holy, and blameless, and above reproach in His sight. When we are one with Christ, married to Christ, and in His body, then we are covered by His glory and righteousness. In Christ, we become blameless, holy, and above reproach. This can happen only in Christ, but outside of Him, we are sinful and dead. ✤ We receive reconciliation by participating in the Mysteries of the Church: In Baptism, we die with Christ and rise with Him; in Confirmation (Chrismation), the Holy Spirit abides in us; in Communion, we are one with Christ. When we participate in His death and resurrection and become members of His Church and abide with Him and He in us, then we can become *"holy, blameless, and above reproach in His sight,"* covered by Him. But St. Paul clarifies an additional condition in the following verse:

1:23 if indeed you continue in the faith, grounded and steadfast. St. Paul teaches the Colossians that they will become *"holy, blameless, and above reproach,"* only if they *"continue in faith."* St. Paul gives them a warning here against apostasy and relapse. They must remain grounded and steadfast in their faith.

and are not moved away from the hope of the gospel which you heard. The hope spoken of here is that which is mentioned above in verse 12, that we

are now *"qualified ... to be partakers of the inheritance of the saints in the light,"* being children of God and eligible for the inheritance of the saints in the light.

which was preached to every creature under heaven, of which I, Paul, became a minister. The hope in being qualified to be partakers of the inheritance of the saints in the light (v.12) is not only for the Jews, but is preached to every person—of every tongue, tribe, and race. Everyone who accepts Christ can retain the same hope. This hope must be preached, which is why Christ sent out the disciples to go and preach the gospel: *"And He said to them, 'Go into all the world and preach the gospel to every creature'"* (Mark 16:15). St. Paul himself was *"appointed"* (Acts 22:10) to spread the gospel when Christ appeared to Him and said the following: *"Rise and stand on your feet; for I have appeared to you for this purpose, to make you a minister and a witness both of the things which you have seen and of the things which I will yet reveal to you. I will deliver you from the Jewish people, as well as from the Gentiles, to whom I now send you, to open their eyes, in order to turn them from darkness to light, and from the power of Satan to God, that they may receive forgiveness of sins and an inheritance among those who are sanctified by faith in Me"* (Acts 26:16-18).

1:24-29 St. Paul begins where he left off in the previous verse, discussing his ministry: *"I, Paul, became a minster."*

1:24 **I now rejoice in my suffrings for you.** Although St. Paul, at the time of writing this epistle, was in prison, he rejoiced in his suffering for them because of the hope of the gospel. The purpose of his *"chains"* (Col. 4:3), he tells the Colossians, is to preach this hope to them. If he is willing to suffer that much, shouldn't the Christians in Colosse walk worthy of this hope and calling? St. Paul expresses that he is happy to suffer for them and that they are now qualified to be partakers of the inheritance of the saints in the light.

and fill up in my flesh what is lacking in the afflictions of Christ, for the sake of His body, which is the church. When St. Paul used the word "afflictions" here, he was not referring to the atoning sufferings of Christ. As a member of the body of Christ, St. Paul's suffering is the sufferings of Christ; our afflictions are Christ's, because we are members of His body. Since many people (until the Second Coming of Christ) will join the body of Christ and be afflicted for Him, then, the afflictions of the body of Christ have not yet been fully realized. St. Paul is ready to fill up what is lacking in the afflictions of Christ, meaning he is willing to endure more suffering. St. Paul is taking his portion in the afflictions of Christ, for the sake of His body, which is the Church. [St. Paul is, thus, in no way expressing any lack in the atoning sacrifice of Christ, but rather is referring to the afflictions of the body of Christ—His Church— which will continue to be filled up until His Second Coming, and of which St. Paul is sharing a portion].

1:25 **of which I became a minister according to the stewardship from God which was given to me for you, to fulfill the word of God.** St. Paul here provides a very good definition of what it means to be a minister. Ministry is a calling and a stewardship. Think of an owner who hires a steward to run his business. Just as that steward does not own the business, we are stewards of God and not the owners. We serve for the sake of the people of God in the form of stewardship, given to the servants for the sake of the people to fulfill the word of God (salvation).

1:26 **the mystery which has been hidden from ages and from generations, but now has been revealed to His saints.** The hidden mystery is that of salvation, especially for the Gentiles. Before, they were alienated and strangers, but now, Christ called them to be in His body. This mystery was hidden in the Old Testament, before Christ, but now it has been revealed to his saints and all believers. This mystery was also made known to those from a Jewish background, that God accepted the Gentiles and made both (Jews and Gentiles) one in His body.

1:27 **To them God willed to make known what are the riches of the glory of this mystery among the Gentiles: which is Christ in you, the hope of glory.** God was pleased to make known to His saints the riches of the glory of this mystery. This mystery is glorious and rich. The riches of the glory of this mystery is Christ Himself. Christ now is among the Gentiles, dwelling among them, and they are the body of Christ. God made known to His people—His saints—the riches of His glory. He is our hope of glory, that we will receive eternal life with Him.

1:28 The servant is responsible for preaching Christ, warning every man, and teaching in wisdom.

Him we preach. (1) of 3. We are to preach Christ, not our ourselves, nor our own ideology, philosophy, or knowledge. No, we should simply preach Christ.

warning every man. (2) of 3. The Greek word translated here as *"warning"* can also be understood as meaning "counseling" (i.e., reasoning with someone, maybe through admonishment or chastising, to urge them to choose the right spiritual and doctrinal substance). We must advise those whom we serve on how they are to walk worthy of Christ's calling.

and teaching every man in all wisdom. (3) of 3. We should focus on keeping the teaching pure.

that we may present every man perfect in Christ Jesus. The purpose of any ministry is to present every man perfect in Christ Jesus: *"Be perfect, just as your Father in heaven is perfect"* (Matt. 5:48). To be perfect is to be in the likeness of Christ: *"For if we have been united together in the likeness of His death, certainly we also shall be in the likeness of His resurrection"* (Rom. 6:5).

1:29 **To this end I also labor, striving according to His working which works in me mightily.** To serve God one must labor, not according to one's own power, but by the power which God supplies, *"striving according to His working which works in me mightily."* We labor and strive in order to preach Christ, teach the truth, and counsel the people, so that we can present every person perfect in Christ Jesus.

Chapter 1 Questions

1. For what three things does St. Paul commend the Colossians?

2. What does St. Paul pray for the Colossians to do?

3. Which verse implies that Jesus is the source and the goal of all creation, and how does the verse give this implication?

4. Who founded the Colossian church

5. What other epistle written by St. Paul is very similar to his epistle to the Colossians?

2

Chapter Outline

- St. Paul's concern for their salvation (1-7)
- Against false theology (8-15)
- Against false spirituality (16-23)

Introduction

St. Paul was concerned about the salvation of the Colossians because of two major philosophical influences: Judaism and Gnosticism. Throughout this chapter, you will find a discussion of some of these influences. St. Paul begins by discussing his concern for the salvation of the Colossians. Then, he elaborates on how we should understand the mystery of God and why it is important to have the true knowledge about this mystery. St. Paul addresses next, the notion of false spirituality. He moves on by explaining to the Colossians their completeness in Christ (outside of whom we are nothing). Finally, he discusses how the cross of the Lord Jesus Christ put an end to the law of the Old Testament.

2:1 **For I want you to know what a great conflict I have for you and those in Laodicea, and for as many as have not seen my face in the flesh.** St. Paul concluded the last chapter by saying, *"To this end I also labor, striving according to His working which works in me mightily."* After saying he strives for them, he wants them to know about a great conflict he has for them. This *"great conflict"* is St. Paul's anxiety or concern about their salvation. So, how do we connect these two verses together (1:29 and 2:1)? Because of this great anxiety and concern in his heart regarding their salvation, he labors and strives in prayer for them. This reminds us of the Lord Jesus Christ, how He labored striving in prayer in Gethsemane. St. Paul, as a father and true shepherd, in his prayer for them, was concerned for their salvation. He is not only concerned about those in Colosse and Laodicea, but also for, as St. Paul says, *"as many as have not seen my face in the flesh."* St. Paul is concerned about all the Gentiles, even those who have never seen him, as he said in his epistle to the Romans, *"For I speak to you Gentiles; inasmuch as I am an apostle to the Gentiles, I magnify my ministry"* (Rom. 11:13); elsewhere he also indicates that he is *"a minister of Jesus Christ to the Gentiles, ministering the gospel of God, that the offering of the Gentiles might be acceptable, sanctified by the Holy Spirit"* (Rom. 15:16). St. Paul is saying that he cares for all the Gentiles, as this is his calling from God. Also, do not forget that St. Paul wrote this letter while he was in prison, so there were many who could not see his face because of this. ❖ This teaches us a lesson: the best antidote for anxiety is prayer. When there is some conflict in our hearts, then when we lift up our hearts and trust Him with our concern,

He will help us.

✠ *False Teaching - Judaism:* ~ The reason for his *"great conflict"* was that their exposure to the false teachings of Gnosticism and Judaism. Many who converted to Christianity, who were formerly adherents of the Jewish religion, taught that Christians needed to keep all the requirements of the law in order to be saved. St. Paul will explain in detail later in this chapter about how the requirements in the law were only *"a shadow of the good things to come, and not the very image of the things"* (Heb. 10:1), which were fulfilled in Christ. That is why we do not have to continue keeping up with the *"shadow."*

✠ *False Teaching - Gnosticism* ~ What about Gnosticism? Gnosis is derived from a Greek word which means knowledge. They were teaching that you can attain salvation by knowledge, not by faith. They had some strange philosophies. For example, they believed that all material was defiled and sinful in itself. Therefore, they did not believe God created material. They taught that there were things that derived from God, but were not equal to Him, things known as "emanations." With each emanation, its status was likewise less and less until material was created at some point. The first emanation from God was, in their view, the Lord Jesus Christ. In this sense, they do not believe in the divinity of the Lord Jesus Christ, but that he is simply a mediator between God and us, like the angels who are mediators. They also believed that it exhibits a lack of humility for us to worship God directly. According to them, true humility is to worship His emanations, such as Christ or the angels. The church in Colosse was exposed to this philosophy and the philosophy of Judaism. St. Paul was concerned for their salvation, and therefore, suffered great anxiety (a *"great conflict"*) because of the fear that the false teachings of Gnosticism and Judaism may interfere with the truth which was delivered to them.

2:2 **that their hearts may be encouraged, being knit together in love, and attaining to all riches of the full assurance of understanding.** How is your heart opened to receive and understand this knowledge of the mystery of Christ? St. Paul is not speaking about intellectual understanding, but rather experiential knowledge. There is a big difference between knowing about God and actually knowing God. The way to grow is to know God and His mystery— we need to live in love of God and one another. When our hearts are united together in the love of God, then our hearts will be encouraged to understand fully the mystery of God. St. Paul is then, saying, "This is my prayer: 'That your heart be encouraged, being knit together in love, by which you will grow and attain the understanding and the knowledge of the mystery of God.'"

This knowledge will make you free and sure of what you have experienced. You will say that the one you know, you have heard and seen yourself (*"I have heard of You by the hearing of the ear, but now my eye sees You"*—Job 42:5). St. Paul is not speaking about just any kind of understanding, but about the *"the full assurance of understanding."* That refers to the notion that you are sure that what you understand is right.

to the knowledge of the mystery of God. St. Paul prays that the Colossians come to the *"knowledge of the mystery of God, both of the Father and Christ"* (Col. 2:2). St. Paul is telling them, if they want to grow in knowledge, let us grow in the true knowledge of God. Gnosticism teaches that knowledge is independent of God and can save you independently of faith. That is, of course, incorrect. True knowledge is of God and Christ

both of the Father. What is the mystery of God? The mystery of God the Father is that He loved us to the end, that He sent His only begotten Son to the world in order to save us. Thus, we are saved because of His love and grace—because He chose to save us, not because we are worthy. God reconciled us to Himself and reconciled the Gentiles to the Jews, the heavenly with the earthly, and man with Himself. That is the mystery of the Father.

and of Christ. The mystery of Christ is that He emptied Himself and died on the cross and accepted to be a curse for us to save us. St. Paul is saying, "I want you to grow in knowledge in order to understand the mystery of God—the Father and Christ. ❖ What then is the difference between the knowledge of the mystery of God and that of Gnosticism? Gnosticism makes knowledge superior to and independent of faith, and thus, it destroys the necessity of faith and all the Mysteries (Sacraments); for example, we are baptized because we have faith in Christ that if we do so, we will be washed from sin and He will make us His children; but if this knowledge is independent from faith, then it destroys the Mysteries of the Church.

2:3 **in whom are hidden all the treasures of wisdom and knowledge.** If you want to come to true knowledge, it is in Christ, *"in whom are hidden all the treasures of wisdom and knowledge."* This verse directly confronts Gnosticism. Compare between the words *"hidden"* and *"mystery,"* and also between *"treasures"* and *"riches."* There are treasures of wisdom and knowledge which are hidden in Christ; that is why it is a mystery. But, once you believe in Him and accept Him and get to know Him, then these treasures will be revealed, which will allow you to gain the riches of the full understanding of the knowledge of the mystery of God.

2:4 **Now this I say lest anyone should deceive you with persuasive words.** We should understand that all the power of Satan lies in his power to deceive. If Satan lost his ability to deceive, then Satan would become powerless. How does Satan induce anyone to fall into sin? It is fundamentally the same way he caused our father and mother (Adam and Eve) to fall into sin through deception (in the Divine Liturgy, the clergyman prays, "when we fell through the deceit of the serpent"). Be aware—and when you listen to any words, try to compare them to the absolute truth of the word of God.

2:5 **For though I am absent in the flesh, yet I am with you in spirit, rejoicing.** St. Paul is saying, although he is absent in the flesh (being in prison in Rome at the time of the writing of this epistle), he is with them in spirit (meaning, his relationship with them is not bound simply by physical presence, but while he is far away, he is, nonetheless, connected to them on a spiritual level). Although he feels a sense of angst over their spiritual wellbeing (having *"great conflict"* as mentioned in Col. 2:1), but he, nonetheless, was happy to hear from Epaphras the good news about the Colossians. ❖ The good news of the flock always brings joy to the heart of the shepherd. When he realizes that his people and flock are growing in their love toward one another and in the knowledge of God, this makes his heart happy and joyful. Thus, although St. Paul was in prison, he was, nonetheless, happy to hear good news about them. That news included that they were in *"good order"* and exhibited *"steadfastness"* of faith in Christ:

to see your good order. *"Good order"* refers to the Colossians as being a well-organized body of Christ. In our physical bodies, everything is organized well and in good working order. Thus, the members in the church at Colosse were in harmony with one another, each doing their part in an orderly way.

and the steadfastness of your faith in Christ. The *"good order"* of the Colossians was the manifestation of their steadfast and strong faith in Christ. From within, they were growing in their faith in Christ, and this was manifested on the outside in their good order. Accepting and receiving Christ should be demonstrated by walking in Him and growing in Him. Thus, *"good order"* is the outward aspect of the Church while *"steadfastness"* is the inner basis on which the Church rests.

2:6-7 **As you therefore have received Christ Jesus the Lord, so walk in Him, rooted and built up in Him.** It is not enough to receive and accept the Lord, but if you truly receive Him, you are to follow Him and this should be manifested in your works. As an analogy, think of a plant; for it to grow, the plant's roots need to dig deep into the ground. In order to walk in Christ, you need to be rooted and built up. *"Rooted"* implies their vitality, like a plant. *"Built up"* is used to metaphorically refer to a mountain or a building with a strong foundation, which, therefore, implies solidity. Thus, *"rooted and built up"* means the church in Colosse expressed vitality and was solidly founded.

and established in the faith, as you have been taught. This faith is that which was passed down from Christ and the apostles. St. Paul is warning them against any new doctrine, as he said in his epistle to the Galatians: *"Even if we, or an angel from heaven, preach any other gospel to you than what we have preached to you, let him be accursed"* (Gal. 1:8). Rejecting any new doctrines is an important element in spiritual maturity and growth.

abounding in it with thanksgiving. The more we grow in our faith, the more we become grateful and give thanks to God. Such gratitude is a sign that one is growing in faith, *"abounding in it with thanksgiving."*

2:8 **Beware lest anyone cheat you.** St. Paul understands how Satan works, which is through deception. There are three channels that St. Paul

delineates as being what Satan uses to deceive us:

through philosophy and empty deceit. (1) of 3. Philosophy's empty deceit, which is not according to Christ, is one avenue by which Satan causes our downfall. True philosophy is the knowledge of God, because in Christ all the treasures of wisdom and knowledge are in Him. But, when we are trying to be wise away from Christ, then we are using earthly measures rather than heavenly ones to gain knowledge. Unfortunately, many students in universities become very confused about faith; many philosophy classes cast doubt on the faith. St. Paul, therefore, warned us against such philosophies.

according to the tradition of me. (2) of 3. Satan sets the tradition of men in opposition of the teachings of Christ as another channel by which he can deceive us. Christ rebuked the religious leaders of Israel because they exalted the traditions of men more than the teachings of God.

according to the basic principles of the world, and not according to Christ. (3) of 3. Satan desires that we think about earthly instead of heavenly things. The Old Testament practices, for example, having been fulfilled in Christ, became simply earthly practices. The empty philosophies of the world comes through the tradition of men and cannot help us go beyond the basic principles of the world (earthly things) and elevate us to what is heavenly (understanding the mystery of God). Although Greece was the source of major philosophers, the cross was foolishness to them, not being able to understand the mystery of the cross, which is the mystery of love (*"We preach Christ crucified, to the Jews a stumbling block and to the Greeks foolishness"*—1 Cor. 1:23).

2:9   For in Him dwells all the fullness of the Godhead bodily. St. Paul here is responding to the heresy of Gnosticism in which they say that Jesus Christ is simply an emanation from God, not God Himself. Thus, he makes clear that in Christ is *"all the fullness"* of the divinity. The essence of the Godhead dwelt in Him. Not only did Christ bear the attributes of divinity, but His very essence was the same as the Father, even as He took flesh and became Man.

2:10   and you are complete in Him. If we are united with Christ, *"in whom are hidden all the treasures of wisdom and knowledge"* (Col. 2:3), then we become complete in Him. Our completeness comes from our union with Jesus Christ, not through philosophy. To be complete and whole, we must abide in Christ.

✤ *True humility* ~ Here St. Paul

gives us a different understanding of humbleness. Many people equate humility with inferiority: they say, "if you want to be humble, then say 'I am nothing, I cannot do anything, I am a failure.'" That is not humility. Humility is knowing that you cannot do anything away from Christ, and also to know that in Christ, you are complete, strong, successful, prosperous, and *"can do all things"* through Him (Phil. 4:13).

who is the head of all principality and power. St. Paul again responds to the Gnostic belief that Christ was like the other emanations of Christ, such as the angels. He is the Head (i.e., the origin and creator) of the angels, not equal or similar to them.

2:11   In Him you were also circumcised with the circumcision made without hands, by putting off the body of the sins of the flesh, by the circumcision of Christ. Here, St. Paul addresses those Christians who were being influenced by Judaism. Although there are some who wanted to impose Jewish practices on Christians, such as circumcision, the Colossians had undergone spiritual circumcision, which is superior to circumcision of the flesh. They were circumcised without human hands, but by God in a spiritual way, *"by putting off the body of the sins of the flesh, by the circumcision of Christ."* In circumcision of the flesh, only the foreskin is shed; but in circumcision of the spirit, the entire body of the sins of the flesh is put off. As clarified in the next verse, this happens through the Mystery of Baptism. We put off the desires of the flesh and our corrupt nature; all of this is being washed away from the person. *"There is also an antitype which now saves us—baptism (not the removal of the filth of the flesh, but the answer of a good conscience toward God)"* (1 Peter 3:21). Since circumcision is a symbol of Baptism, which was performed on the eighth day, therefore too, Baptism of infants is appropriate (as has been occurring since the beginning of Christendom). (For more on Baptism and its relation to circumcision, see also Rom 2:28-29; 1 Cor. 7:19; Gal. 5:6, 6:15; Phil. 3:3)..

2:12 **buried with Him in baptism, in which you also were raised with Him through faith in the working of God, who raised Him from the dead.** In Baptism, we die with Christ and we are also raised with Him. You accept Baptism because you believe in God, that He will put off the body of sin in the water of Baptism, having *"faith in the working of God."* You believe that God will give this water the power of regeneration and that He will raise you from death through Baptism. *"Therefore we were buried with Him through baptism into death, that just as Christ was raised from the dead by the glory of the Father, even so we also should walk in newness of life"* (Rom. 6:4). This is why we baptize with total immersion

(as it is in accordance with the apostolic teaching), "burying" the person under the water and raising him or her out of the water.

2:13 **And you, being dead in your trespasses and the uncircumcision of your flesh, He has made alive together with Him, having forgiven you all trespasses.** St. Paul reflects further on the work of Baptism in the Colossians. Previous to their Baptism, they were dead because they were sinners when they were Gentiles; they also had not put off the old flesh and corrupt nature (the old man—Rom. 6:6; Eph. 4:22). God the Father made them alive by forgiving them all their trespasses on the cross. Thus, the power of Baptism comes from Christ's death on the cross. This power, which we receive in the water of Baptism, has its origin in the mystery of the cross.

2:14 **having wiped out the handwriting of requirements that was against us, which was contrary to us.** Christ forgave all our trespasses on the cross, of which we receive the benefit through Baptism. We, then, live within the period of the New Testament, no longer having to fulfill *"the handwriting of requirements that was against us."* The laws of the Old Testament had requirements. If a person sinned, there were a number of things that had to be done in order to attain righteousness. Otherwise, the person is condemned and is dead. When Christ came, He fulfilled all the requirements of the law on our behalf and *"wiped out the handwriting of requirements that was against us."* Whenever we used to break the law in the Old Testament, it was as if there was a handwritten record against us which indicated that we were dead eternally. Christ fulfilled the requirements of the law and wiped out the handwritten record of requirements. The law was not only *"against us"* by its demands, it was also *"contrary to us"* by its accusation.

And He has taken it out of the way, having nailed it to the cross. Christ took the requirements out of our way, like a veil that separated us from God which had to be torn (cf., Matt. 27:51; Mark 15:38; Luke 23:45). The Lord reconciled us with the Father by fulfilling the requirements of the law, wiped out the handwritten record of requirements against us, and removed it from the middle. Christ carried our sin and became a *"curse for us"* (Gal. 3:13), and nailed the curse of the broken law ("the handwriting of requirements that was against us") to the cross. ❖ This imagery is used by St. Paul to bring to people's minds the ancient tradition of canceling bonds by striking a nail through the writing.

2:15 **Having disarmed principalities and powers, He made a public spectacle of them, triumphing over them in it.** Not only did the Lord Jesus Christ forgive our sins and wipe out the handwritten record against us, but He also disarmed Satan and his soldiers. *"Disarming"* them conjures up the notion of taking their weapons away and exposing what Satan and his army were using against us. Now we are empowered by the grace of God and can crush Satan under our feet (cf., Rom. 16:20) through the power of the cross (cf., Acts 26:18). As a conqueror, God made a public spectacle of him, making a show of his captives and putting them to shame.

2:16 **So let no one judge you.** Now that Christ has put an end to the law, St. Paul is saying that no one should judge the Colossians for not ascribing to the Jewish laws and religious customs.

in food or in drink. This relates to what the Jewish law prescribes (for example, Lev. 7:10-27). St. Paul is indicating that such requirements have come to an end.

❖ *This prohibition is not about fasting* ~ St. Paul speaks here of Jewish traditions, not the Christian concept of fasting. Some people use this verse against fasting. Fasting is a commandment of Christ, and it is the practice of the Church in the New

Testament. St. Paul is not attacking here the tradition of Christ or His doctrines, but rather the Jewish traditions, to which the Lord put an end and replaced by the doctrines of Christianity. To respond to the claims against New Testament Christian practices (such as fasting), simply look at the next verse and see how St. Paul clarifies that these things are a *"shadow of things to come."* They are part of the Old Testament and not referring to Christian teachings and customs. St. Paul was against the *"shadow,"* not the fulfillment of the shadow.

or regarding a festival. Here, St. Paul refers to Jewish celebrations, generally.

or a new moon. The Jews in the Old Testament were told to observe the first day of each month (Num. 28:11), which is yet another requirement that St. Paul is saying is no longer necessary for Christians.

or sabbaths. The observance of Saturday as the pinnacle holy day of the week for the Jews was overshadowed by Sunday as being the Lord's day (the day Christ resurrected).

2:17 **which are a shadow of things to come, but the substance is of Christ.** In Judaism, there were many things which were a symbol or type of things to come, and thus, after Christ fulfilled the Old Testament, we were

no longer required to continue in such things. We do not observe the Passover, the Feast of Tabernacles, etc. We are to pay no attention to the shadows since Christ (the true Antitype) has come, but to observe what we find in Him and the gospel. Think of a person and a shadow cast as he walks. The *"substance"* of the shadow is the person who is walking. Likewise, the shadow is not the object of our interest anymore, but the person who makes its substance—the Lord Jesus Christ.

cheat. This is the third time in this chapter that St. Paul tells the Colossians not to be deceived or cheated (Col. 2:4, 8, 18).

2:18 **Let no one cheat you of your reward.** St. Paul is telling the people of Colosse to be careful lest Gnosticism or Judaism deceive them and cheat them of their reward. It is simply a tradition, philosophy, and wisdom of men, not of God.

taking delight in false humility and worship of angels. As discussed previously, Gnosticism taught that we are not worthy to worship God Himself and thus we are to worship His emanations such as the angels. From outside it looks like humility, but this is outward humility, not genuine humility.

intruding into those things which he has not seen. Gnostics proclaimed special revelations that were simply imaginations of their mind. They are not things that they claim to have actually seen, but things they just imagine.

vainly puffed up by his fleshly mind. Regarding the philosophy of Gnosticism, when I start trusting in my own wisdom, I will be puffed up by my carnal and fleshly mind, thinking I am humble when in reality I am trusting my wisdom, not the wisdom of God. In the Magnificat (Luke 1:46-55), St. Mary spoke about God saying, *"He has scattered the proud in the imagination of their hearts"* (Luke 1:51). Thus, when a person is *"puffed up,"* they will be inclined to consider their imaginations as revelation and teach them to people as such. (Regarding not being wise in one's own eyes, see Prov. 3:7; Rom. 11:25, 12:16).

2:19 and not holding fast to the Head. A person who does not hold fast to Christ (the Head) is set loose to pride himself on things which he has not seen. Such a person who is not conformed to Christ will trust his own mind and heart.

the Head, from whom all the body, nourished and knit together by joints and ligaments, grows with the increase that is from God. Christ is the source of our nourishment, our union, and our growth. From Him, the entire body is nourished, knit

together (expressing our union) by the different members of the Church (joints and ligaments), and in Him, we will grow. If someone teaches you false spirituality or teachings (such as false humility and the worship of angels, including this which he has not seen because of the pride of their mind), this indicates he or she is not holding fast to the Head (i.e., Christ).

2:20 Therefore, if you died with Christ from the basic principles of the world, why, as though living in the world, do you subject yourselves to regulations. St. Paul is wondering why, if the Colossians died in Baptism, they are going back to the basic principles of the world and the earthly Jewish traditions (which are simply the *"shadow of things to come"*—Col. 2:17). It is as if they are still living in the world and their mind is not on heavenly things. Once we are baptized, we become heavenly beings, not earthly ones, living according to heavenly requirements, not earthly, and according to the substance, not the shadow. St. Paul reminds them of their heavenly status.

2:21-22 **"Do not touch, do not taste, do not handle," which all concern things which perish with the using—according to the commandments and doctrines of men?** All of these things that we *"touch"* or *"taste"* or *"handle"* will eventually perish with the using of it. St. Paul asks them to think about the spiritual kingdom of God and whether it consists of these worldly things. Thus, Christ said to the disciples, *"Not what goes into the mouth defiles a man; but what comes out of the mouth, this defiles a man"* (Matt. 15:11). Sins come from one's heart, such as adultery, cursing, idol worshipping—those things defile a man. All the prohibitions about food and such are *"according to the commandments and doctrines of men."* We must follow the commandments of God rather than those of men.

2:23 **These things indeed have an appearance of wisdom in self-imposed religion.** God is not the author of these traditions, but rather the tradition of men. It has from the outside an appearance of wisdom (do not touch this, taste that, handle this), but it is self-imposed religion. It is *"self-imposed"* because it is not imposed by God, but rather by men.

false humility, and neglect of the body, but are of no value against the indulgence of the flesh. Because of the belief of the Gnostics that sin is inherent in the material substance of the body, therefore, the only way by which perfection can be reached is to punish the body by asceticism, so through the infliction of pain and the mortification of the flesh, the region of pure spirit may be reached, and thus, man may be etherealized and become like God. St. Paul said that these things are not from God. God wants us to nurture our bodies and take care of them so that we can worship Him. The Gnostic mindset of treating the body as sinful is of no value to a person who is trying to inhibit the indulgence of the flesh and has no efficacy in overcoming the lusts of the flesh. Many people keep these traditions but cannot control the lusts of the flesh. St. Paul differentiates between true spirituality and false spirituality. False spirituality pleases one's ego, but true spirituality seeks to please God. False spirituality is to submit to one's self (self-imposed religion), but true spirituality is to submit to the doctrine of God. False spirituality has no value in disciplining the flesh, but true spirituality teaches self-control.

Chapter 2 Questions

1. In Colossians 2:8, St. Paul warned the Christians in Colosse so that they would not fall prey to certain things. What were those things?

2. What did St. Paul mean when he said of Christ, "In Him dwells all the fullness of the Godhead bodily" (Col. 2:9)?

3. In Colossians 2:11, St. Paul spoke of how Christians had been "circumcised with the circumcision made without hands." What did he mean by that?

4. St. Paul told the Colossians about a "handwriting of requirements" that Christ had "wiped out" (Col. 2:14). How did Christ blot it out?

5. St. Paul taught that we should not allow anyone to judge us (Col. 2:16). Explain the context of his statement.

3

is, sitting at the right hand of the Father.

Chapter Outline

• New life with Christ (1-4)
• Putting off the old man (5-11)
• Putting on the new man (12-17)
• Life application (18-25)

Introduction

After explaining our completeness in Christ in the previous chapter, St. Paul continues here to reflect on our new Christ. Christ said that He came that we *"may have life, and ... may have it more abundantly"* (John 10:10). We need to put to death the old man and all his actions, then we must put on Christ with all the deeds of the new man. St. Paul will eventually discuss some practical application of this.

3:1-4 In these verses, St. Paul mentions some important facts. (1) In Baptism, we died ("for you died") and "were raised with Christ." (2) Our lives are hidden with Christ (which will be explained further below). (3) Christ will appear and we will appear with Him in glory. (4) With all these three points in mind, St. Paul asks us to set our minds on things above, seeking that which is from above. (5) The reason we should set our minds on things above and not on earth is because that is where Christ

3:1 **If then you were raised with Christ.** St. Paul is saying that, with Christ, there has to be a real change in our lives after Baptism. How do we die with Christ and rise with Him? This happened in Baptism, which St. Paul spoke about in the previous chapter when discussing the *"circumcision made without hands"* being *"buried with Him in Baptism, in which, you also were raised with Him"* (Col. 2:11-12). If you were really raised with Christ and really died with Him, then where is Christ now? He is in heaven. Thus, we have to seek things which are above (seek heavenly things), and set our minds on heavenly things. A person may seek heavenly things without setting his or her mind on things above. That is not enough. Setting our minds means being preoccupied with heavenly matters.

seek those things which are above. The fact that Christ is in heaven means when we die in the flesh, we will go to heaven to be with Christ, only if we are with Him here while we are on earth. *"If anyone serves Me, let him follow Me; and where I am, there My servant will be also. If anyone serves Me, him My Father will honor"* (John 12:26). Also, we read in the Book of Revelation, *"To him who overcomes I will grant to sit with Me on My throne, as I also overcame and sat down with My Father on His throne"* (Rev. 3:21). Thus, as the Son is sitting at the right hand of the Father, so we will be sitting with Him in heaven.

3:2 Set your mind on things above, not on things on the earth. Not seeking earthly things does not mean ignoring our responsibilities here on earth. However, while we are carrying out our earthly responsibilities, we are to be preoccupied with our home. Think of the ambassador who lives in a foreign country but all his work and priorities are for his country. Thus, *"we are ambassadors for Christ"* (2 Cor. 5:20), dealing with our responsibilities here, but in everything, working for our home in heaven. Not seeking earthly things means setting our priorities straight according to God's will: *"Seek first the kingdom of God and His righteousness, and all these things shall be added to you"* (Matt. 6:33).

3:3 For you died, and your life is hidden with Christ in God. In another letter of St. Paul, he said, *"It is no longer I who live, but Christ lives in me"* (Gal. 2:20). Thus, I am hidden in Christ. When people look at me, they should see Christ, not me. If you remember how Christ's life was like on earth, He emptied Himself, He had no place to lay His head; from the outside, there was no luxury of life, although from within, there was glory and true joy and happiness. If our lives

are hidden with Christ, this means we will not have a life which seeks luxury and glory, but we will be like Christ, carrying our crosses and suffering with Him, although from within, we will have peace and joy. Christ died and was persecuted, and thus, we will also be persecuted and suffer with Him (*"If indeed we suffer with Him, that we may also be glorified together"*—Rom. 8:17).

3:4 When Christ who is our life appears, then you also will appear with Him in glory. In His Second Coming, Christ will appear in glory, and we too will appear with Him in glory. If our lives are now hidden with Christ, then later, our lives will be revealed in glory. If we participate in His suffering here on earth, then we will participate in the glory of His Second Coming. Recall that during the Transfiguration of Christ, Moses and Elijah both appeared with Him in glory as well.

Christ who is our life. St. Paul used a very nice term here about Christ. If you want to appear with Christ in glory, then you need to make Christ your life. As St. Paul said, *"It is no longer I who live, but Christ lives in me"* (Gal. 2:20). When Christ is my life, I will appear with Him in glory. Ask yourself, is Christ your life or not? ✠ That is why in Baptism, it is death with Christ. We die to the world and we have no life here any longer. In Baptism, we die to the world in order to live for Christ. St. Paul is now reflecting on the true understanding of asceticism. If you recall in the prior chapter, St. Paul addressed the issue of false asceticism. Now, he speaks about true asceticism, which is to die with Christ and experience His suffering in our lives. Definitely, when we know that we will appear with Him in glory and sit on thrones with Him in Heaven, this should be great motivation for us to die with Christ and suffer for Him now

3:5 Therefore put to death your members which are on the earth. What does this mean? Does St. Paul want us to kill our bodies? Actually, in answering those questions, we may refer to the terms that St. Paul used when he spoke about the carnal person and the spiritual person (Rom. 8:5-7). The carnal person is the one who is lead by the desires of the flesh, while the spiritual person is led by the Spirit. St. Paul is saying, if your members are controlled by the earthly desires, then your members belong to earth. If, however, your members are controlled by heavenly desires, then your members are spiritual and you are a spiritual person. In this verse then, St. Paul means that we should put away the earthly and evil desires and keep them from working in our bodies and controlling our members. Furthermore, St. Paul provides examples of things that should not prevail in our bodies:

fornication, uncleanness, passion, evil desire. St. James said in his letter that sin starts with evil desire: *"Each one is tempted when he is drawn away by his own desires and enticed. Then, when desire has conceived, it gives birth to sin; and sin, when it is full-grown, brings forth death"* (James 1:14-15). Once we are preoccupied with our evil desires, we will then gain a *"passion"* for it. When I become passionate about evil desire, then I will defile myself (which is *"uncleanness"*). If I defile myself, I may then commit sins with others (which is *"fornication"*). St. Paul can be considered to have delineated a progression: evil desire, passion, uncleanness, and fornication.

and covetousness, which is idolatry. *"Covetousness"* is a broader term than it may seem. It is to show a great desire for something that is not yours. Thus, a person may covet his brother's wife, possessions, and other belongings. Therefore, the most destructive evil desire is covetousness, which is idolatry. Instead of worshipping (and desiring God), you are worshipping (or desiring) an idol. If you are heavenly, then you should seek things that are above (Col. 3:2). If, however, you are earthly and your members are on earth instead of heaven, then, you will covet earthly things and will develop evil desires which will lead to a passion for such things, uncleanness, and eventually even fornication. Covetousness is idolatry because it is as if you are denying God and worshipping another idol (whatever it is you covet).

3:6 Because of these things the wrath of God is coming upon the sons of disobedience. If I start to worship another idol, not God, then I am disobeying God. I become a son of disobedience, not a son of God. What will I reap? St. Paul answers, *"The wrath of God."* It is as if St. Paul is saying, "If you do not understand your calling and that you are a heavenly being, then let me give you another reason to motivate you to be so: consider the wrath of God. If the love of God is not enough for you, then maybe the wrath of God will encourage you to live a life of repentance." (*"The fear of the LORD is the beginning of wisdom."*—Psalm 111:10).

3:7 in which you yourselves once walked when you lived in them. The Colossians understood what St. Paul meant in the previous verse because they previously walked in such passions. St. Paul is telling them and reminding them that although they were once sons of disobedience, now they are sons of God and should not turn back to their former ways. In their Baptism, they promised to leave their former lives and to accept the calling to live as children of God. Their former lives should have been buried in Baptism.

3:8 But now you yourselves are to put off all these. St. Paul here gives us another list that is distinct from the one he gave in verse 5 (see above). However, the word *"all"* refers to the previous list and the list about which he is to relay.

put off. St. Paul used two metaphors in this chapter. The first was when he said, *"put to death your members"* (verse 5). Repentance is putting to death our sinful ways. The second is here where he said *"put off,"* as if the old man is a garment you take off and in its place you put on the garment of the new man, which is Christ (*"Put on the new man which was created according to God, in true righteousness and holiness."*—Eph. 4:24). St. Paul is saying that, as a new creature in Christ, you are to put off all these sins, which he lists below:

anger. All of us, at certain moments in our lives, become angry. Anger is energy which can be destructive or constructive. That is why we need to manage our anger in order for it to be edifying rather than destructive. Here, St. Paul is referring to destructive anger.

wrath. This is the explosion of anger. Far from being constructive, this is when anger has exploded and turned into yelling, screaming, threatening, and maybe even physical violence. Often, wrath comes in a hierarchical way, from those with authority to those who are under their authority.

malice. When a person becomes angry and then wrathful, he may develop malice in his heart and his standards may become malicious. Malice includes conspiring against people, intending to hurt others, and relaying evil towards them. A person will develop such things when he is bitter on the inside.

blasphemy. This refers to resisting others, such as when the Bible teaches us not to blaspheme against the Holy Spirit, which means we are not to resist the Holy Spirit (Matt. 12:31). Thus, this word includes the notion of resisting others and their goodness, or resisting something positive that happened to them, and even denying their rights.

filthy language out of your mouth. This is often the result of someone who is angry and wrathful. Also, if someone is unclean from within, what will come out is filthy language.

3:9 **Do not lie to one another, since you have put off the old man with his deeds.** St. Paul is saying that lying is an action of the old man. Many consider that lying is not telling the truth, but if you think about it, we lie a lot, without even realizing it or paying heed to it. Many times we give the "perfect" answer, although it is not the real and most honest answer. To what extent are you honest and real in your relationships with others? If we are Christian and have put off the

old man, then we need to be real and honest, speaking only the truth (cf., Eph. 4:15). Many times, we only say what others want to hear to please them, being hypocrites, and thinking that this is wisdom for how we should approach others.

3:10 **and have put on the new man who is renewed in knowledge according to the image of Him who created him.** The sins listed above are the deeds of the old man which we put off in Baptism. Thus, how can we walk with such sins if we have put off the old man? In Baptism, we have put on the new man, and this new man grows from one stage to another in the likeness of God (which is why he said, "renewed in knowledge according to the image of Him who created him"). Thus we are to grow from glory to glory to reach the likeness of God.

renewed in knowledge. The renewal mentioned here is *"in knowledge."* The word Metanoia is the word for repentance in Greek. This word is composed of two words: *"Meta,"* which means change, and *"Noia,"* which refers to the mind. Thus, Metanoia is the changing or renewal of the mind. St. Paul is speaking here of the renewal of one's mind to acquire the mind of Christ rather than the mind of the old man (*"For 'who has known the mind of the LORD that he may instruct Him?' But we have the mind of Christ."*—1 Cor.

2:16). Thus, as it is said in Romans 12:2, *"Be transformed by the renewing of your mind."* The process of the new man growing from one stage to another to the likeness of God begins with the renewal of the mind. That is why St. Paul tells us later in this chapter, *"Let the word of Christ dwell in you richly"* (v.16). When the word of Christ dwells in my heart, it will renew my mind and I will be transformed; that is why the Lord said, *"You are already clean because of the word which I have spoken to you"* (John 15:3).

✠ *It is important to attend the readings of the Divine Liturgy in order to take communion* ~ The notion of attending the readings in order to take communion is not just meant to make you come early, but there is a deeper meaning. You need to attend the readings because the readings will purify your heart; then, you will be in a clean stage and worthy to partake of His precious body and blood.

renewed ... according to the image of Him who created him. St. Paul is saying to the Colossians that they are children of God and therefore, since children usually look like their parents, so too, they must now look like God. If we are children of our creator, we should retain the image of the One who created us. In this way, people will look at us and say they see the reflection of God's image on us.

3:11 **where there is neither Greek nor Jew, circumcised nor uncircumcised, barbarian, Scythian, slave nor free, but Christ is all and in all.** The renewal, of which is spoken in the previous verse, is available to everyone and anyone who accepts Christ. It is different than in the Old Testament at which time only the people of Israel were the chosen people of God. Since Christ is all and in all, anyone who accepts Christ to be in him and that Christ be all things for him, then he will acquire this renewal and transformation, of which is spoken in the previous verse.

3:12-17 In the previous set of verses (5-11), we read about how we should put off the old man and put to death our members. Now, St. Paul will explain the other aspect of the new life in which a baptized Christian lives, which is putting on the new man.

3:12 **Therefore, as the elect of God, holy and beloved.** St. Paul describes the children of God with three terms: elect, holy, and beloved. You chose Christ to be your God and your life; that is why He elected you for the inheritance of heaven. This election is based on the foreknowledge of God. We read of this in the Gospel according to John: *"But as many as received Him, to them He gave the right to become children* *of God, to those who believe in His name, who were born, not of blood, nor of the will of the flesh, nor of the will of man, but of God [in Baptism]"* (John 1:12-13). (Also St. Paul tells us, *"For whom He foreknew, He also predestined to be conformed to the image of His Son, that He might be the firstborn among many brethren."*—Rom. 8:29). God elected you to be holy like Him, since you are His children. This holiness and election is not based on our righteousness or worthiness, but rather His grace. All that we do is accept Him. Because of His grace, He will transform you to be holy like Him. Hence, we are beloved because of the grace of God, not because of our worthiness. You may see a child and will love the child especially when they exhibit positive behavior. *"But God demonstrates His own love toward us, in that while we were still sinners, Christ died for us"* (Rom. 5:8). He chose us while we were unworthy; but out of love, He bestowed His Grace upon us.

put on. St. Paul is going to mention virtues that we should *"put on"* in lieu of the sinful ways which we should have *"put off"* since Baptism. Note that the following relate to our dealings with one another. If you are transformed and renewed in the image of God, this will then be manifested in your relationship with others. If you say you are godly, yet you have many problems and issues with others, then you cannot claim to truly be transformed.

tender mercies. When someone refers to a part of the body as being *"tender,"*

it means that part is sensitive to pain. Similarly, when we have a tender heart and tender mercies, we will feel the pain of others and will bestow mercy upon them.

kindness. This describes one's character as being sympathetic, exuding compassion on others, and sharing in the joy of others. When people see such a person, they will describe that person as being kind..

humility. Why did St. Paul mention humility here? Later, St. Paul will speak about husbands, parents, masters, and all such people who have authority. Authority, however should make someone more humble since it was granted to him or her not to control others, but to serve them in love. If we are transformed to the image of Christ, then any authority given to us should be utilized with love for the benefit and service of those for whom we are responsible, *"Just as the Son of Man did not come to be served, but to serve, and to give His life a ransom for many"* (Matt. 20:28).

meekness. This is to be patient and endearing with others. It requires a balance between strictness and looseness, saying the truth without harshness, *"but speaking the truth in love"* (Eph. 4:15). .

longsuffering. This is to be patient with others, not to be impulsive and act out immediately. See how patient God is with His creation. Think of the ones that blaspheme and sin against Him, and yet, how patient God is. As we are children of God, we must likewise be patient and longsuffering. Jonah the Prophet said to God, regarding his assuredness that He would forgive the people of Nineveh if they would repent from their ways, *"I know that You are a gracious and merciful God, slow to anger and abundant in lovingkindness, One who relents from doing harm"* (Jonah 4:2).

3:13 **bearing with one another, and forgiving one another, if anyone has a complaint against another; even as Christ forgave you, so you also must do.** St. Paul elaborated a bit about *"bearing with one another, and forgiving one another."* All of us commit sins in our lives, and thus, we all need forgiveness; and if we need forgiveness, then we should understand the need to be forgiving. In any relationship, both persons will sin. No one can claim they have never sinned against someone else or never hurt anyone. If all of us then commonly hurt others, then we need to be forgiving towards one another, just as we ourselves need forgiveness. If you have a complaint about someone, remember how Christ could have many complaints about you because of sins; but, Christ responded to these complaints by forgiving us all our debts. Christ told us each time we pray, we should ask God to *"forgive us our debts as we forgive our debtors"* (Matt.

6:12; He goes on to warn us about the penalty of not forgiving others: *"For if you forgive men their trespasses, your heavenly Father will also forgive you. But if you do not forgive men their trespasses, neither will your Father forgive your trespasses."*—Matt. 6:14-15). If we have any issues with someone else, we must put on tender mercies, kindness, humility, meekness, longsuffering, and bear with one another and forgive.

3:14 **But above all these things put on love, which is the bond of perfection.** Above all the virtues mentioned previously, we must *"put on love, which is the bond of perfection."* Love is that which will instill mercy, kindness, humility, and longsuffering. When we have love in our hearts, then, we will develop all of these virtues, because love *"is the bond of perfection."* ❖ As explained earlier, the Colossians were dealing with the heresy of Gnosticism, which taught that perfection could only be attained by knowledge. St. Paul, however, responds by declaring that perfection is in love. Here, I recall what St. Paul mentioned in his letter to the Corinthians, *"Knowledge puffs up, but love edifies"* (1 Cor. 8:1).

3:15 **And let the peace of God rule in your hearts.** Can you imagine, if we developed all of these virtues and expressed them to one another? Do you think we will have conflicts and trouble with one another? No, but rather we would be living in peace. When you acquire these virtues, you are letting the peace of God rule in your hearts. If you do not seek to maintain those virtues, then you are, in actuality, pushing peace away; and then, you wonder, why am I not at peace?

to which also you were called in one body; and be thankful. Here, St. Paul reminds us that we are called to be members in the same body, and thus, we are to live in unity. Think of your own body: if its members were not in harmony, imagine the repercussions. However, when everything works harmoniously together, then, there is peace and health. Similarly, we are members in one body, the body of Christ; and when we live in peace with one another through the development of virtues through love which is the bond of perfection, then, we will be fulfilling our calling. In this way, we will be thankful. Just as a person who is thankful to God for health, so too, will we be grateful for a peaceful life amongst the members of the body of Christ.

3:16-17 What picture is St. Paul portraying for us? If you think about it, is this not reminiscent of the Liturgy? In the Liturgy, there are readings from the Scriptures whereby we receive *"the word of Christ."* During the service, there is a time set apart for a sermon where one may receive *"teaching and admonishing."* *"Psalms and hymns and spiritual songs"* are sung during the Liturgy for the purpose of teaching, by which we can learn and also be admonished. All present during the Divine Liturgy join in *"singing with grace in [their] hearts] to the Lord."* In whatever we do in the Liturgy, we should be doing *"in the name of the Lord Jesus"* and *"giving thanks to God the Father through Him."* The term "Eucharist," which refers to the body and blood of Christ, is derived from the Greek word which means "giving thanks." This passage can be said to be the image of the worshipping Church in the Divine Liturgy.

3:16 **Let the word of Christ dwell in you richly in all wisdom.** We cannot put on virtues (such as those mentioned in the preceding verses) without the word of God. If the word of God dwells in you richly, you will be able to pursue and flourish in virtue. God's word is able to save us, as St. James tells us: *"Therefore lay aside all filthiness and overflow of wickedness, and receive with meekness the implanted word, which is able to save your souls"* (James 1:21). The word of God is also the *"power of God to salvation for everyone who believes"* (Rom. 1:16). It is also able to edify us and transform us in wisdom. When the word of God dwells in us richly, we will be transformed. ❈ It is truly destructive when we separate ourselves from the word of God. St. Paul did not say "read the gospel" or *"read the word of God."* No, rather, he said, *"Let the word of Christ dwell in you richly."* The word of God is meant to dwell inside you, and not just that, but to dwell richly. Many people have a difficult time to recall verses from the Bible, which can be an indication that the word of God is not truly dwelling inside them richly. On the other hand, if the word of God dwells in you richly, you will naturally utter psalms, hymns, and words from the Bible. Think about St. Mary's prayer when the Archangel Gabriel announced to her the good news (Luke 1:46-55). Each aspect of her prayer can be cross-referenced to the Old Testament Scriptures.

teaching and admonishing one another. How does a person teach and admonish others? We should not rely on our own understanding but rather extract teaching and admonishment from the word of God. This cannot happen unless the word of God dwells in you richly, and this also requires wisdom in order to decipher the word of God properly. ✤ We have a responsibility to one another to teach and admonish one another.

in psalms and hymns and spiritual songs, singing with grace in your hearts to the Lord. When the word of God dwells richly in us, from without, we will be speaking the word of God, and from within, we will be singing with grace to the Lord. We will be able to engage in continuous prayer with God so that in all times our hearts will be praying to Him.

3:17 **And whatever you do in word or deed, do all in the name of the Lord Jesus, giving thanks to God the Father through Him.** St. Paul here declares a very important rule for all Christians. Whatever you say or do, it must be said or done in the name of the Lord Jesus Christ. Moreover, all such actions should be endowed with a sense of gratefulness and thanksgiving. If we remember this rule, to say and do all things in His name and with thanksgiving, then our lives will truly be transformed.

3:18-24 In this set of verses, St. Paul lends a practical application of the principals delineated in the previous sections. Each of the people addressed in these verses have a place of authority and a correlating person with lesser authority: husbands and wives, parents and children, masters and servants. The teaching here is that God has allowed certain people to have authority, not for the purpose of ruling over and controlling others, but rather to serve them in love. Those with such authority need to grow in humility, recalling that Christ came to serve, not to be served (Matt. 10:28). Research (from a non-religious background) even tells you that the best type of leadership is that which involves serving others. ❈ On the other hand, all submission is to God, not to the authority figure. I submit because God asked me to submit. Thus, I submit to the word of God through the person who has authority. Submission will be for my glory. Thus, while all authority is humbling, all submission is glorious.

3:18 Wives, submit to your own husbands. If you want to be glorified, submit to your husbands. This is a submission of love, not the submission of slaves. When St. Peter spoke about this, he said this is how *"the holy women who trusted in God also adorned themselves, being submissive to their own husbands"* (1 Pet. 3:5).

as is fitting in the Lord. This phrase can be understood in two ways. First, it is fitting for wives to submit to their husbands. Second, submission is fitting if it is *"in the Lord"*; that is, such submission is fitting if it is in obedience to God and not contrary to Him, since otherwise *"we ought to obey God rather than men"* (Acts 5:29).

3:19 Husbands, love your wives and do not be bitter toward them. If you are the head and are given authority, you are not to use your authority to rule over and abuse your wives, but rather you are called to love your wife and not to be harsh ("bitter") toward her. Therefore, *"Husbands, love your wives,*

just as Christ also loved the church and gave Himself for her" (Eph. 5:25).

❈ *Women need love, and husbands seek respect* ~ Why did God ask wives to be submissive and husbands to express love? It is because women need love and husbands need respect. That is why God gave this commandment, to suit our needs.

3:20 Children, obey your parents in all things, for this is well pleasing to the Lord. If you want to please God, obey your parents. If you want to cause God to be disappointed with you, then disobey your parents. It is very simple. You cannot pick and choose in what you will be obedient, but rather children are called to be obedient *"in all things."*

3:21 Fathers, do not provoke your children, lest they become discouraged. While children are asked to be obedient to their parents, on the other hand, parents must not use their authority to provoke their children. You need to be kind. Remember that authority has been given to you to serve your children in love. Children may become discouraged and fail due to the parents' exercise of authority in the wrong way.

3:22 Bondservants. Christianity does not encourage slavery (just as it does not encourage any other type of abusive relationship which befalls anyone). St. Paul, however, addresses those who are already in the predicament of slavery, not encouraging the practice. If a person is in a country where slavery is approved, then the question is how does a person in that situation act in a Christian manner?

obey in all things your masters according to the flesh. The bondservants are called to be submissive, and thus they should be obedient to their masters. St. Paul makes it clear that the masters are simply *"according to the flesh"* because they actually only have one master, and that is Christ Jesus. However, according to the country and system in which they lived, there was slavery, and thus, these masters (who were not their true masters) deserved obedience.

not with eyeservice, as men-pleasers, but in sincerity of heart, fearing God. This obedience can be one of two things. We can apply this to the obedience of children to their parents, employees to their bosses, and anywhere else. Many people today obey *"with eyeservice"*: if the person of authority sees me, I will follow all the rules, but when they are not looking, I will not. Think of the example of someone driving on the road: the way you drive when a police car is next to you is quite different than when there

is none. Do not simply seek to please men. If you have the fear of God in your heart, you will do it with sincerity of heart and with God in mind, not men.

3:23-24 And whatever you do, do it heartily, as to the Lord and not to men, knowing that from the Lord you will receive the reward of the inheritance; for you serve the Lord Christ. Submission should not be contingent on whether those with authority over you are watching or not, because God is watching and He is the one who will reward you. The earthly reward is nothing, but rather, you should be seeking the heavenly reward, as St. Paul tells us earlier in this chapter (*"Seek those things which are above, where Christ is, sitting at the right hand of God. Set your mind on things above, not on things on the earth."*—Col. 3:2-3). The earthly master cannot reward you heavenly, but only God. Thus, when you do everything heartily, you will receive your reward. *"Whatever you do, do it heartily, as to the Lord and not to men."*

3:25 But he who does wrong will be repaid for what he has done. If you choose to do wrong and serve with *"eyeservice"* and be a men-pleaser instead of serving with the fear of God, then, you will be repaid for whatever you have done, for there is no partiality.

3:22 **and there is no partiality.** St. Paul does not simply address servants, but in the beginning of the next chapter, St. Paul will address masters as well.

Chapter 3 Questions

1. What are the two sings that you are raised with Christ?

2. In what way is our life hidden with Christ?

3. Why should we put to death our members on earth? (Two reason)

4. What are the characteristics of the new man?

5. Does St. Paul encourage slavery?

6. Why should bondservants obey their masters?

4

Chapter Outline

- Instructions to masters (1)
- Prayers (2-4)
- Proper conduct (5-6)
- Greetings (7-14)
- Concluding remarks (15-18)

4:1 Masters, give your bondservants what is just and fair, knowing that you also have a Master in heaven. St. Paul concluded the previous chapter by giving instructions to different people with different roles. That last instruction given was to bondservants, and since with God *"there is no partiality"* (Col. 3:25), St. Paul continues here by instructing masters about their role. ✤ In the Roman empire, slavery was approved, and people were divided into masters and bondservants. Masters, at that time, used to deal very harshly with bondservants. Actually, they used to consider their servants as property, and the law gave them authority over their servants. For example, if any master killed or tortured his servant, no one would hold him accountable or question him. That is why in dealing with masters, St. Paul gave them four important instructions. First, he tells them to deal with them in equality, although the societal system at that time

treated servants as second-class and as the property of their masters; no, they are brothers and should be treated as such. Second, St. Paul wants masters to treat them as fellow humans who have feelings and who will suffer from mistreatment; thus, they should not be dealt with harshness. Third, St. Paul urges masters to treat their servants fairly and justly; for example, if they do something positive they should be rewarded, and if they do something wrong, the discipline should not be excessive, but should be guided by the principles of fairness and justice. Fourth, St. Paul wants masters to keep in mind that they themselves are bondservants to the heavenly Master; thus, masters should remember that God will deal with them in the same manner in which they dealt with their own servants.

✤ *This verse is applicable to anyone in a place of authority* ~ You may think that since, today, slavery is not generally accepted or practiced, then, this verse is not applicable to us. However, anyone in a place of authority can apply this verse to him or herself. For example, if you are a boss at your job and you have people working under your authority, do not deal with them harshly or with unfairness and injustice; remember that Christ said, *"For with the same measure that you use, it will be measured back to you"* (Luke 6:38). Just because people are under your authority does not mean they are lesser than you. If you are in a position of authority, please remember that God gave you this authority not to rule over others, but to serve with love, kindness, mercy, justice, and fairness.

4:2-4 St. Paul relates six important elements of prayer:

4:2 Continue. (1) of 6. When St. Paul says *"continue,"* he is teaching us that we need to be consistent in prayer. Many times, we pray for a few days and then stop praying for a while in a repeating cycle. Such inconsistency weakens our prayers. If you want to benefit and grow in the life of prayer, the first piece of advice we can derive from St. Paul is to be consistent. *"Pray without ceasing"* (1 Thess. 5:17) is the same instruction that our Lord Jesus Christ gave to us (cf. Luke 18:1-8— *"men always ought to pray"*).

earnestly in prayer. (2) of 6. This refers to prayer with passion. Some people just recite the words of prayer with their mouths while their hearts lack passion. St. Paul is teaching us that we must accompany prayer with sincere and intense conviction (unlike the hypocrites: *"These people draw near to Me with their mouth, and honor Me with their lips, but their heart is far from Me"*—Matt. 15:8). Many times, when we sing songs in church, such as before a meeting or at other times,

people do not participate; and even if they do participate, when they sing, it lacks passion. When we praise the Lord, it should be accompanied with fervency. In the Monday Psali of the Midnight Praises, we say, "Gather all of my senses, to praise and glorify, my Lord Jesus." So actually in this Psali, I am calling all of my senses to be gathered together to bless the name of my Lord Jesus Christ.

being vigilant in it. (3) of 6. Vigilance in prayer can be understood to mean paying attention and not to be distracted during prayer. Many people complain about such distractions; for example, they wonder if they said all the parts of their prayer that they had planned, or maybe they left something out. Such people are focused on reciting the prayer but are not vigilant in understanding it.

with thanksgiving. (4) of 6. One of the fathers said, "There is no gift without increase, except the one without thanksgiving." The Church teaches us to give thanks to God for every condition, concerning every condition, and in every condition. Every time we pray, we start with thanksgiving. Even in the funeral prayers in the Coptic Orthodox Church and in the Sacrament of the Unction of the Sick, the first prayer is the Prayer of Thanksgiving. We give thanks always because we trust that whatever God allows or whatever He does for us is for our benefit. Thus, we thank Him always. (See also Luke

17:15-18; Eph. 5:20; 1 Thess. 5:16-18; furthermore, His Holiness Pope Shenouda III wrote a book entitled "Life of Thanksgiving.")

4:3 **meanwhile praying also for us.** (5) of 6. Yes, you should pray for yourself, but do not forget to also pray for others. When we pray for others, it is as if we are putting the interests of others before our own. That is real love, as we read in 1 Cor. 13:5, love *"does not seek its own."* (St. Paul also teaches us elsewhere, *"Let each of you look out not only for his own interests, but also for the interests of others."*— Phil. 2:4). God appreciates when we pray for others before ourselves. As St. Paul seeks prayer *"for us,"* we learn that among the others, we should also pray for the servants who should have a high priority in our prayers. That is why in the litanies of the Coptic Orthodox Church, we pray for our patriarch, bishops, priests, deacons, and all the servants and ranks of the Church. This is because they preach the gospel of Christ and need assistance in their ministry. It is like Joshua and the Israelites who were in war against Amalek while Moses was on the mountain praying for him *"And so it was, when Moses held up his hand [in prayer], that Israel prevailed; and when he let down his hand, Amalek prevailed"* (Ex. 17:11). Maybe you are not a Sunday school servant or have a particular assigned ministry in the

church, but the one thing each of you can do is pray for the servants. . .

that God would open to us a door for the word. (6) of 6. As we are asked to pray for the servants of the gospel, we should know that the goal of the ministry is to preach Christ and His word. We should never be distracted from this goal, but rather, the main ministry of the Church is to preach Christ to everyone. That should be our focus. ✦ Note that some deacons change the prayer during the Litany of the Gospel from, "Pray for the Holy Gospel" to "Pray for the spreading of the Holy Gospel." In actuality, this is a prayer for one element of the gospel, while at the same time, there are many other aspects of the gospel about which we should be praying as well. It is, therefore, better to keep this prayer as is. ✦ With regard to praying for the gospel, we can learn several reasons from St. Paul why we should do so. "That God would open to us a door for the word." Who will prepare the people and open the door before the servants of Christ to go and preach?

to speak the mystery of Christ. God is the one who will do that. Also, we pray that when the servant preaches, they do not preach from their own experiences, but rather *"to speak the mystery of Christ."* St. Paul explains that phrase elsewhere (Eph. 3:4), which we understand to refer to the mystery of love: how God loved us, reconciling us with Him, and reconciling the Gentiles with the Jews (cf., Rom. 16; Eph. 1:9, 3:3, 9; Col. 1:26, 2:2). We pray that God reveals His love to every person.

for which I am also in chains. Usually with service, there is a cross and suffering. We read about this in Sirach 2:1: *"My son, if you presented yourself to serve the Lord, prepare yourself for many afflictions and hardships."* Hence, we should pray for the servants. St. Paul himself tells us that he wrote this letter while he was *"in chains."* Servants, therefore, need prayer that God would give them the patience and strength to endure suffering and to carry their cross joyfully without losing hope or falling into despair.

4:4 that I may make it manifest, as I ought to speak. Sometimes we filter our speech and do not present the gospel in the right way. For example, many people interpret the Bible differently, and thus, when they manifest the gospel, they do so in the wrong way. For example, if someone preaches there is no need for Baptism, Communion, and Confession in order to be saved; although they utilize Scripture, they are preaching it in the wrong way. We should all pray for the gospel to *"make it manifest, as I ought to speak"*; that is, in the proper way, as God wants me to preach it, not simply as I want to preach.

4:5-6 St. Paul now addresses the Colossians regarding how they should maintain proper conduct with others, especially with the unbelievers ("those who are outside"). St. Paul gives us five important points for how to deal with people who are not members of the Church:

4:5 Walk in wisdom toward those who are outside. (1) of 5. Many times when we hear of incidents against Christians, and more specifically, persecution of the Copts in Egypt, we are incited and act out upon such news unwisely--passionately, but without wisdom. Before you act, you must evaluate whether the action is wise or is not; and whether it is according to the will of God or not. The measure of wisdom is not by earthly standards, but rather by heavenly ones. One of the major characteristics of wisdom, as St. James describes it to us, is that we are *"peaceable"* ("But the wisdom that is from above is first pure, then peaceable, gentle, willing to yield, full of mercy and good fruits, without partiality and without hypocrisy."—James 3:17).

✤ *Practical application from the story of a Khalifah and a Christian* ~ I am sure (if you are Coptic) that you have heard of the miracle of the moving of the Moqattam Mountain. Do you know how this miracle started? The Khalifah (also written as Caliph, which is a title for the chief Muslim and religious leader regarded as the successor of Islam's first leader, Muhammad), had a Jewish minister. He called one of the Christian leaders in order that he may debate with the Jewish minister. When the debate began, the Christian leader said to the Khalifah, "How do you want me to debate with those who were described as being less than an animal?" While the Jewish minister was insulted, the Christian leader clarified, "Does it not say in the prophecy by Isaiah, '*Hear, O heavens, and give ear, O earth! For the LORD has spoken: "I have nourished and brought up children, and they have rebelled against Me; the ox knows its owner and the donkey its master's crib; but Israel does not know, my people do not consider"*'" (Is. 1:2-3). This irritated the Jewish minister and in response he said to the Khalifah, "They have a verse in the Bible that says, 'If you have faith as a mustard seed, you will say to this mountain, *"Move from here to there,"* and it will move; and nothing will be impossible for you' (Matt. 17:20). If they do not move a mountain, then their Book and faith is wrong, and thus, they should all either convert to Islam or be killed. Why am I telling you this story? With all due respect to this Christian leader, I do not think that the approach which he used was wise. Because he did not use a wise approach with *"those who are outside,"* he brought this big trial and hardship on the whole Coptic Church. But because *"God is love"* (1 John 4:8) and covers a multitude of sins (cf., 1 Pet. 4:8), He delivered the Church from this great tribulation that befell it.

redeeming the time. (2) of 6. In his letter to the Ephesians, St. Paul related wisdom to redeeming the time. *"See then that you walk circumspectly, not as fools but as wise, redeeming the time, because the days are evil"* (Eph. 5:15-16). Thus, we learn that one of the ways that we present ourselves as wise to those who are outside is by redeeming the time. This refers to using our time effectively in what edifies, not wasting our time in idle or even destructive activities. When people from the outside see that everything you do is for edification, building up one another, advancement, and progress, then, they will perceive you as being wise and desire to imitate your wisdom. ✠ This phrase also means that we should not simply be conformed to *"those who are outside"* (the non-Christians) and spend time with them in nonsense or ungodly activities. No, we should we redeem the time. Although we should walk with them, we are not to engage in activities that are not beneficial and not constructive.

4:6 Let your speech always be with grace. (3) of 5. There is a big difference between speaking gracefully and speaking judgmentally. You need to learn how to speak *"with grace."* Grace is love, forgiveness, acceptance, and being non-judgmental. God spoke with grace with the woman who was caught in the *"very act"* of sin and condemned by the Pharisees (John 8:3-4). God spoke with grace to Zacchaeus (Luke 19) and the man who was a paralytic for 38 years (John 5), as well as with the Samaritan woman (John 4). Let me give you an example of speech which lacks grace and is rather judgmental—that of Simon the Pharisee speaking judgmentally about Christ who accepted the endearing gestures by the woman who was a sinner: *"Now when the Pharisee who had invited Him saw this, he spoke to himself, saying, 'This Man, if He were a prophet, would know who and what manner of woman this is who is touching Him, for she is a sinner'"* (Luke 7:39). In St. Peter's first epistle, we read, *"If anyone speaks, let him speak as the oracles of God. If anyone ministers, let him do it as with the ability which God supplies, that in all things God may be glorified through Jesus Christ, to whom belong the glory and the dominion forever and ever. Amen"* (1 Peter 4:11). Speaking gracefully is to speak the word of God. Think of how St. Mary and St. Elizabeth greeted one another (Luke 1:40-55). Elizabeth told her, *"Blessed are you among women, and blessed is the fruit of your womb! But why is this granted to me, that the mother of my Lord should come to me?"* (Luke 1:42-43). Therefore, when you deal with *"those who are outside,"* we should not speak judgmentally or as though we are better than them, but rather with love and acceptance. Yes, we judge the action, but not the person. Christ exhibited

this throughout His life, such as when He exhibited love and acceptance to the Samaritan woman, although He did not approve of her actions. In this manner, she repented and turned her life around.

seasoned with salt. (4) of 5. When we add salt to food, we do so to give it a better taste and also as a preservative. In the same way, when our words are seasoned with salt, then, when the people hear what we say, it will be pleasant and not merely offensive. Whenever Christ spoke to a particular individual, He never offended him or her. Although when He spoke generally to people such as the Pharisees, He kept reiterating *"Woe to you"* (for example, in Matt. 23); yet, when Christ spoke one-on-one with even the same Pharisees, He never spoke with words meant to offend anyone. Even when Simon the Pharisees spoke to himself expressing judgmental thoughts about Christ, the Lord responded by simply telling him a story: *"Jesus answered and said to him, 'Simon, I have something to say to you'"* (Luke 7:40). Christ continued, *"There was a certain creditor who had two debtors. One owed five hundred denarii, and the other fifty. And when they had nothing with which to repay, he freely forgave them both. Tell Me, therefore, which of them will love him more?"* (Luke 7:41-42). When Simon answered and said, *"I suppose the one whom he forgave more,"* Christ applauded him saying, *"You have rightly judged"* (Luke 7:43). That is graceful speech. Christ pointed out Simon's mistake, but did so by delineating the actions of Simon that were lacking, rather than the person of Simon: *"You gave me no water for My feet, ... You gave Me no kiss, ... You did not anoint My head."* Christ was very careful not to offend Him. ✤ Moreover, the words given should not destroy others but rather preserve their souls. Some people use words that are sharper than a sword which hurt and destroy. St. Paul says, however, that we should preserve people's souls by what we speak: *"Let no corrupt word proceed out of your mouth, but what is good for necessary edification, that it may impart grace to the hearers"* (Eph. 4:29). The purpose of even our admonishment is not simply to punish or be destructive, but rather to preserve their souls.

that you may know how you ought to answer each one. (5) of 5. We must learn how to deal with everyone according to each person's own particular needs. You need to change your pattern and style of relating to others according to the one with whom you speak. For example, you may have a number of two or three children, but the way you handle each one may be very different. A clever physician does not prescribe the same medication for everyone, but will give the right medication to each person as is necessitated by each one's individual predicament.

4:7-8 Tychicus, a beloved brother, faithful minister, and fellow servant in the Lord. Tychicus was mentioned in both Acts 20:4 and also Eph. 6:22. St. Paul uses such endearing words whereby we can deduce his genuine and sincere feelings towards those who served with him. He considered them not simply as disciples but as equals: *"beloved brother"* and *"fellow servant."*

will tell you all the news about me. I am sending him to you for this very purpose, that he may know your circumstances and comfort your hearts.... They will make known to you all things which are happening here. By these verses, we understand that both Tychicus and Onesimus were the carriers of this letter, taking it from Rome to Colosse and the people in Laodicea. We can deduce four other tasks they were assigned to accomplish: (1) Quelling any concerns about St. Paul's situation—relaying news about how he was doing; (2) Sharing what was happening in Rome with regard to the church there and the persecution of Christians as well; (3) Learning the circumstances of the church in Colosse and nearby cities. As a father, St. Paul was concerned and wanted to know how they were doing in the spiritual path, especially considering the concerns over the influence of heresies such as Gnosticism which may have impacted them; (3) Comforting the hearts of the recipients of this letter. It is important that the servants share news, communicating amongst each other, to their coordinators, to the priests, and to the bishops. Such communication comforts the hearts and keeps the unity of the Church intact. When we know each other's circumstances, we will pray for one another and will pray for each other.

4:9   with Onesimus, a faithful and beloved brother, who is one of you.   Onesimus is Philemon's bondservant and the primary subject of whom St. Paul writes in his epistle to Philemon. After he stole some money from Philemon and fled, he somehow came in contact with St. Paul while he was imprisoned in Rome, and through whose teachings, he became Christian (which is why St. Paul writes, *"I appeal to you for my son Onesimus, whom I have begotten while in my chains"*—Philem. 10). Evidently, Onesimus began to serve with St. Paul, as indicated by the fact that he was designated (along with Tychicus) to send this letter to Colosse on his behalf. Although a bondservant of Philemon, St. Paul describes him as a counterpart in the flock of Christ: *"a faithful and beloved brother, who is one of you."* When St. Paul says that Onesimus is *"one of you,"* we understand also that he was living in Colosse as was Philemon.

4:10-11   St. Paul now mentions three Jewish fellow workers: Aristarchus, St. Mark, and Barnabas.

4:10   Aristarchus my fellow prisoner greets you.   Aristarchus is mentioned in Acts 19:29. He was imprisoned in Rome, which some say was not imposed on him but rather something he sought willingly to remain with St. Paul in his prison. The first imprisonment in Rome was like house arrest (Acts 28:30). For example, when Pope Shenouda was exiled to the monastery, the monks who were in the monastery with him could not leave either.

with Mark the cousin of Barnabas. This is St. Mark, the one who established the Coptic Church in Alexandria, Egypt. Although he is mentioned here as being the cousin of Barnabas, he was his nephew in actuality; the term cousin was loosely applied in this situation maybe because they were close in age, as may happen in modern days. (The Greek word used here to signify the family relationship between Barnabas and Mark can be understood to mean nephew. In many translations, such as the King James Version and also the Arabic translation of the Bible, the term used is "sister's son" in lieu of cousin.).

(about whom you received instructions: if he comes to you, welcome him).   It is interesting when you read about what St. Paul says regarding St. Mark here. Recall that there was some tension in the relationship with St. Mark, who St. Paul refused to take with him along for his second missionary trip (Acts 15). Now it appears that this tension was over, not only describing him as one of the *"fellow workers for the kingdom of God,"* but also instructs the recipients of this letter to *"welcome him"* if they were to see him. This teaches us a lesson about tension between servants that may develop. Sometimes, it takes people years to resolve their issues in their hearts, if ever. Here, we see St. Paul and St. Mark resolved their tension expediently and genuinely. We even read St. Paul writing to St. Timothy, that St. Mark *"is useful to me for ministry"* (2 Tim. 4:11).   .

4:11 and Jesus who is called Justus. Justus's original name was Jesus. However, after the ascension of our Lord Jesus Christ, people did not feel it was proper that he keep that name; and it was, therefore, changed.

These are my only fellow workers for the kingdom of God who are of the circumcision. The only three Christians who were *"of the circumcision"* (from a Jewish background) that attended to the needs of St. Paul were Aristarchus, St. Mark, and Barnabas.

4:12-13 Epaphras, who is one of you, a bondservant of Christ, greets you, always laboring fervently for you in prayers, that you may stand perfect and complete in all the will of God. For I bear him witness that he has a great zeal. If you remember, Epaphras was the bishop of Colosse who preached Christianity to them. St. Paul spoke of very highly of him because he was very zealous in his service. He is described as *"a bondservant of Christ"* (that is, completely and willingly submitting to Christ). The description of Epaphras here is the description also of a faithful servant. We should examine ourselves against these words. Do we labor fervently in prayer for those whom we serve? Epaphras prayed consistently and with passion that his flock is *"perfect and complete in all the will of God."* He also exhibited *"great zeal."* Some people today likewise serve in such a manner, whose passion you can feel, while others serve out of routine and in a very lukewarm way. You must put all of your heart in your service. In Jeremiah 48:10, we read, *"Cursed is he who does the work of the Lord negligently."* If you are called to serve the Lord, you must have passion to serve the Lord with fervor.

for you, and those who are in Laodicea, and those in Hierapolis. Colosse, Laodicea, and Hierapolis were three cities which in today's terms can be considered like the diocese over which Epaphras the bishop served.

4:14 **Luke the beloved physician and Demas greet you.** While we learn here that Luke is regarded as *"beloved"* and is known for being a *"physician,"* we do not read mention of a single word about Demas. Eventually, as we read in his epistle to St. Timothy, St. Paul tells us, "Demas has forsaken me, having loved this present world." One may deduce that at the time of the writing of this epistle, St. Paul began to notice that the heart of Demas was not like before (cf., Philem. 24) and that his sincere love of the service was becoming lukewarm. This shows us that St. Paul does not simply complement people insincerely or in a hypocritical manner; rather, he honestly described people in his letters.

4:15 **Greet the brethren who are in Laodicea, and Nymphas and the church that is in his house.** After sending greetings from the people who were with him, St. Paul turns his attention to greeting recipients of his letter. Christians in Laodicea used to meet in the house of a person named Nymphas. The houses of all believers should be houses of God, and we should all have prayer corners in our houses, as if we have a *"family altar"* in each of our houses.

4:16 **Now when this epistle is read among you, see that it is read also in the church of the Laodiceans.** St. Paul is telling them, "When you read this letter in Colosse, make sure you take this letter and have it read also in Laodicea."

and that you likewise read the epistle from Laodicea. Most of the scholars of the Bible say that the letter *"from Laodicea"* is the letter of St. Paul to Ephesus. Note, as mentioned previously in this commentary (in the introduction), the letter to the Colossians and the letter to Ephesus are very similar to each other; however, the letter to the Ephesians was focusing on the Church as the body of Christ, while the letter to Colosse was focusing on Christ as the Head of the Church.

4:17 **And say to Archippus.** We read in Philemon that St. Paul addressed his letter *"to Philemon ..., to the beloved Apphia, Archippus ..., and to the church in your house."* Many scholars, along with St. John Chrysostom (in Homily 1 on Philemon), believe that Apphia was Philemon's wife, and Archippus was his son.

"Take heed to the ministry which you have received in the Lord, that you may fulfill it." Apparently, Archippus was beginning to drift a little from her fervency in ministering for the Church, and therefore, St. Paul is sending him this message, which shows us that the members of the Church have a responsibility to one another to hold each other accountable. In this message to Archippus, we can learn many lessons. (1) It is God who gives us our ministry. (2) We need to fulfill the ministry. (3) We need to be watchful and vigilant in order to fulfill our ministry. Every servant in any capacity can regard this message to Archippus as being a message to him or her personally. When you give account before God on the last day for your service, you will be able to say to Him, "I made profit with the talent that you gave me" (cf., Matt. 25:14)..

4:18 **This salutation by my own hand—Paul. Remember my chains. Grace be with you. Amen.** With all of St. Paul's letters, he would dictate the letter to someone who would then write the letter down for him; St. Paul himself, however, would sign it at the end. Recall that St. Paul was in prison at this time, and thus, while signing this letter he was doing so while he was literally in chains. That is why he said specifically, *"This salutation by my own hand—Paul."* He is saying this was his authentic signature, but the signature of the letter was done so while he was chained, and therefore, he asks the recipients of this letter to remember his predicament.

Chapter 4 Questions

1. How should masters deal with their bondservants? Why?

2. What are the requirements for sincere prayer?

3. How should we deal with "those who are outside"?

4. What is the message that we get from St. Paul's final greetings?

5. Why did he not mention a word about Demas?

6. What are the qualifications of a servant?

St. Paul's First Epistle to the
Thessalonians

AUTHOR: St. Paul. St. Paul is the author of this letter. Although the letter to the Thessalonians begins, "Paul, Silvanus, and Timothy, to the church of the Thessalonians," Silvanus and Timothy are mentioned not as authors, but rather to signify that they were fellow co-workers in establishing the church in Thessalonica (cf., Acts 17).

PLACE & TIME: This letter was written while St. Paul was in Corinth, sometime around 50-51 AD, during his second missionary trip. Biblical scholars almost unanimously agree that this was the first letter written by St. Paul (among the ones known to us) and that it is possibly the earliest writing in the entire New Testament.

THEME

The theme of this letter is about holiness in view of Christ's coming. When Christ's return to judge the world is kept in mind, it is expected that the manner in which we live our lives will be focused on preparing ourselves for His Second Coming. This epistle, then, deals with how to live our lives as a preparation for eternal life.

PURPOSE

St. Paul wrote this first letter to the Thessalonians to support and encourage them to remain steadfast in the faith—praising them for their endurance and maintaining their faith. He also instructs them on how to live a holy life, walking worthy of their calling. Furthermore, St. Paul wanted to give them hope by writing to them about the Second Coming of our Lord Jesus Christ, and to comfort them about those who had passed away, particularly those who died as martyrs due to the persecutions they faced.

BACKGROUND & RECIPIENTS

St. Paul, Silvanus, and St. Timothy began to preach in Thessalonica (also known as Thessaloniki, which is situated in present-day Greece), leading to the foundation of a church there around 50 AD, during St. Paul's second missionary trip. The Thessalonian church consisted mostly of Gentiles who experienced persecution from fellow citizens (not from Jews directly, although they were to blame for stirring Gentiles against the new Thessalonian Christians). For that reason, and in accordance with the persuasion and advice of many, they left Thessalonica and went to Berea. When St. Timothy joined them again in Athens, St. Paul sent him to Thessalonica in order to see how the believers in the city were doing, especially in light of their hardships and persecutions. St. Timothy brought back good news to St. Paul indicating that the Thessalonians were very strong in their faith, which delighted the heart of St. Paul.

OUTLINE OF 1 THESSALONIANS

Chapter 1
• Salutation (1)
• Thanksgiving (2-4)
• Their reception of the gospel (5-7)
• Their reputation in every place (8-10)

Chapter 2
• The proper attitude of the servant (1-12)
• The fruits of his ministry (13-16)
• St. Paul's concern for them (17-20)

Chapter 3
• Timothy's visit (1-5)
• Timothy's report (6-11)
• St. Paul's prayer (12-13)

Chapter 4
• Walking in holiness (1-7)
• Walk in love (9-10)
• Walk in diligence (11-12)
• Walk in hope (13-18)

Chapter 5
• The Second Coming (1-3)
• Walk in light (4-11)
• Walk in obedience (12-22)
• Concluding remarks (23-28)

1

Chapter Outline

• Salutation (1)
• Thanksgiving (2-4)
• Their reception of the gospel (5-7)
• Their reputation in every place (8-10)

1:1 Paul, Silvanus, and Timothy, To the church of the Thessalonians. With the exception of Hebrews, it is the custom in all of St. Paul's letters for him to begin by mentioning his authorship (as well as others who may be participating in his ministry) and then following that by identifying the letter's recipients.

Silvanus. He is the same person known elsewhere throughout the Scripture by the name Silas.

in God the Father and the Lord Jesus Christ. St. Paul says this because any Church is founded in God and in His son the Lord Jesus Christ. Christ is the foundation and cornerstone of every church (*"Now, therefore, you are no longer strangers and foreigners, but fellow citizens with the saints and members of the household of God, having been built on the foundation of the apostles and prophets, Jesus Christ Himself being the chief cornerstone, in whom the whole building, being fitted*

together, grows into a holy temple in the Lord, in whom you also are being built together for a dwelling place of God in the Spirit"—Eph. 2:19-22; see also Matt. 21:42; Mark 12:10; Luke 20:17; Acts 4:11; 1 Pet. 2:6-7). St. Paul reminds the Thessalonians that they are the church of God and therefore, the Lord Christ's people, children, and bride.

Grace to you and peace from God our Father and the Lord Jesus Christ. If the Church is founded in God and His son Jesus Christ, then, it is from the Father and the Lord Christ that we receive grace and peace. These are the most needed gifts for any believer. Without God, we cannot achieve anything, but *"the things which are impossible with men are possible with God"* (Luke 18:27); therefore by God's grace we can *"do all things through Christ who strengthens me"* (Phil. 4:13), and *"by grace you have been saved through faith"* (Eph. 2:8). Peace is needed because we are living in the middle of a stormy world in which we suffer hardships and tribulations; therefore, we should seek *"the peace of God, which surpasses all understanding, [which] will guard your hearts and minds through Christ Jesus"* (Phil. 4:7). ❈ When we pray for ourselves and our children, pray that God gives us and them peace and grace, because we all need those gifts.

1:2 **We give thanks to God always for you all.** As mentioned previously, St. Timothy returned from Thessalonica with a good report of how the Thessalonians remained steadfast in their faith although they were embittered by hardships and persecutions. The heart of pastors or servants is made glad when they see the children whom they serve succeeding in their spiritual lives, being confirmed in the faith (cf., 1 Cor. 1:6), conducting their life in holiness (cf., Heb. 12:14). St. Paul was very joyful upon hearing the news of the spiritual wellbeing of the Thessalonians. Instead of looking at his own efforts, St. Paul directs his gratitude to God; it was not his effort, but rather the grace of God helped them in supporting them with grace and relaying upon them peace so that they *"received the word in much affliction, with joy of the Holy Spirit"* (1 Thess. 1:6).

making mention of you in our prayers. The word "priest" refers to one who serves as an intercessor for the people. The proper place of the priest is the altar praying for his congregation.

1:3 **remembering without ceasing.** Whether you are a priest or bishop, Sunday school servant or parent, you should not stop or cease from praying for the ones whom you serve. Samuel the prophet said, *"As for me, far be it from me that I should sin against the LORD in ceasing to pray for you; but I will teach you the good and the right way"* (1 Sam. 12:23; see also Col. 1:9). He felt that ceasing to pray for his people would be a sin against God. The true pastor always prays for those whom he pastors.

your work of faith, labor of love, and patience of hope. St. Paul indicates that he remembers constantly how the Thessalonians exhibited the three pinnacle virtues: *"faith, hope, love, these three; but the greatest of these is love"* (1 Cor. 13:13). Notice in this verse that for each of these virtues, St. Paul added a word—as a qualifier, associated with them: *"work of faith, labor of love, and patience of hope."* When we think of these three virtues, we must think of them in this way. (Also see 1 Thess. 1:9 below).

work of faith. As St. James said, *"faith without works is dead"* (James 2:20). He analogizes faith without works to be like a physical body without a spirit: *"For as the body without the spirit is dead, so faith without works is dead also"* (James 2:26). If we remove works from faith, then faith is dead. That is why St. Paul phrased it in this way; remember the works demonstrated by their faith: *"I will show you my faith by my works"* (James 2:18).

labor of love. St. John implores, *"My little children, let us not love in word or in tongue, but in deed and in truth"* (1 John 3:18). Love must be demonstrated with labor, as is the common saying: "Actions speak louder than words." Some people may never say the words "I love you," yet their love will be clearly exhibited in their actions, while there are many who use the word love and yet do not genuinely love at all as reflected by their actions. (See also John 14:23, 15:12; Gal. 5:13; Eph. 5:2; 1 Cor. 13; Rom. 14:15; 1 John 3:16; note that St. Paul uses similar phrasing about love in Hebrews 6:10: *"For God is not unjust to forget your work and labor of love which you have shown toward His name, in that you have ministered to the saints, and do minister."*

patience of hope. If you have hope, you will be patient and wait until this hope is fulfilled. Thus, hope is demonstrated by patience. What causes an ill person to maintain their regimen involving taking medicine and undergoing tests and treatment? It is the hope of recovery and healing. Thus, their patient endurance in expectation of achieving what they seek reflects the extent of their hope. *"Hope that is seen is not hope; for why does one still hope for what he sees? But if we hope for what we do not see, we eagerly wait for it with perseverance"* (Rom. 8:24-25.

in our Lord Jesus Christ. Here, we are introduced to a very important concept: our hope is in the Lord Jesus Christ. Many people say, "I cannot overcome this sin," or, "I feel it is hopeless to think our family conflict will be resolved," or, "I have no hope in my son returning to God and repenting one day." I would respond, "I agree with you that you cannot have hope in yourself, or your family, or in your son; but, our hope is in the Lord Jesus Christ who can actually change our hearts and transform our lives." While *"with men this is impossible, but with God all things are possible"* (Matt. 19:26). God is the hope of the hopeless and the help of the helpless, as we say in the Litany of the Sick.

in the sight of our God and Father. The work of faith, labor of love, and patience of hope which we exhibit is not before men but rather *"in the sight of our God."* It is He who bears witness of our actions. Many people may praise us, but the most important question is whether God sees our actions and is pleased with them. Does God see my faith working, the laboring of my love and the patience of my hope? That is what matters.

1:4 beloved brethren. Notice the endearing terms used by St. Paul with his flock, demonstrating how a pastor should view his relationships with his people. That is the bond of love (cf., Col. 3:14) which unites all of us together.

knowing ... your election by God. Deciphering the meaning of *"election"* in this verse requires us to delve into theology: in the New Testament, did God choose and appoint individuals who would be regarded as His special people? St. Paul answered this question in his letter to Romans, Chapter 8. The election of God is based on his foreknowledge. God foreknew those who would accept and believe in Him, and those people are elected by God. In the Old Testament, God elected Abraham because he was the only one who accepted and remained faithful to Him. God elected Moses, Elijah, and so many others. Nowadays, the elect of God are the ones who chose God first. It is, thus, your choice whether you will be among the elected or not; if you accept God and become faithful to him, then you will know you are elected to inherit the kingdom of God and receive His inheritance (cf., Gal. 4). All of us are elected, but the question is, do we make our election permanent or not?

1:5-7 St. Paul focuses on how the Thessalonians received the gospel and how it should be preached. We can take these verses as a lesson for how we should relay the message of the gospel to others, delineating five points. I hope that every priest and Sunday School servant keeps these five points in mind and abides by them in their service when they preach the word of God.

1:5 **For our gospel did not come to you in word only.** (1) of 5. The word. This is the explanation of the gospel. It is our responsibility to make the word of God understood clearly. Whether you are a pastor, Sunday School servant, or a parent, it is your responsibility to explain the word of God and communicate it with clarification.

but also in power. (2) of 5. In power. If your actions are not consistent with your words, then the word will lose its power. You preach with power when you, yourself, are living the word of God which you preach. Declaring the word of God by our mouths and then manifesting those words in the way we live every day will present God's word with power (cf., 2 Tim. 1:14; 1 John 1:3).

and in the Holy Spirit. (3) of 5. The Holy Spirit. When you preach, you have to get on your knees and pray for the word of God, asking the Holy Spirit to work in the words that you utter so that it is not your own words from simply your own personal experiences or thoughts but rather expressing the word of God.

and in much assurance. (4) of 5. Assurance. This refers to confidence in the word of God, trusting that it is the absolute truth. We should never doubt the word of God, which has been the tactic of Satan since the time he spoke with Eve until the present. Many people who teach about the word of God or focus on biblical criticism cast doubt on the word of God, but the true pastor and servant of word is assured and confident in the absolute truth of the Scripture; if God said so, then it is so.

as you know what kind of men we were among you for your sake. (5) of 5. The attitude of the servant. Are you willing to endure, suffer, and carry your cross for the word of God? Which attitude do you have when you preach the word of God?

1:6 And you became followers of us and of the Lord, having received the word in much affliction, with joy of the Holy Spirit. The Thessalonians received the word with affliction (with the patience of hope), and yet also with joy. They were convinced that the word they received was not from men but from God. Also, the grace of God and His peace (for which St. Paul prayed) allowed them to receive the word of God with joy although they were bearing much affliction. Having received the word of God, the Thessalonians became followers of the Lord Jesus Christ and His apostles (the icons of Christ), following in their footsteps.

1:7 so that you became examples to all in Macedonia and Achaia who believe. After receiving the word of God, imitating the Lord and His apostles, and incorporating it in their daily lives, the Thessalonians started to become examples to others. When you keep the word of God in your life and apply it, then, you yourself will be an example to others. You are the fifth gospel, preached without the necessity of speaking, but simply by acting in accordance with God's word. In the Divine Liturgy, before reading the Divine Gospel, we read from the Synaxarium, which presents us with stories of saints who embodied the living application of the word of God.

1:8 For from you the word of the Lord has sounded forth, not only in Macedonia and Achaia, but also in every place. Your faith toward God has gone out, so that we do not need to say anything. Many were speaking about how the Thessalonians were steadfast in the word of God and endured much affliction and persecution (even to the point of martyrdom) for the sake of the Lord Jesus Christ. This news *"sounded forth"* in Macedonia, Achaia, and every place, so that many resounded the reputation of the Thessalonians. This further reflected on the reputation of the apostles themselves who preached to them in faithfulness, having preached God to them in the proper way resulting in the proper fruit. In this way, the apostles *"need not to say anything"* about the faith of the Thessalonians since their actions spoke louder than words.

1:9 For they, themselves, declare concerning us what manner of entry we had to you. People who heard about the Thessalonians were testifying about the ministry of the apostles in regard to the manner by which the apostles preached the word of God (see verse 5 above).

and how you turned to God from idols. (1) of 3. This is the work of faith, believing in God to whom they turned as they forsook idol worship (see v.3 above).

to serve the living and true God. (2) of 3. This is the labor of love, worshipping God in word and in deed (see v.3 above).

1:10 and to wait for His Son from heaven. (3) of 3. This exhibits their patience of hope, waiting for Christ's Second Coming.

whom He raised from the dead, even Jesus who delivers us from the wrath to come. Our faith is based on the truth of the resurrection of the Lord Jesus Christ. *"If Christ is not risen, then our preaching is empty and your faith is also empty. Yes, and we are found false witnesses of God, because we have testified of God that He raised up Christ, whom He did not raise up—if in fact the dead do not rise ... And if Christ is not risen, your faith is futile; you are still in your sins"* (1 Cor. 15:14-15, 17). Christianity is based on the doctrine of the resurrection, because this means He will deliver us from the wrath to come. Having risen from the dead, He gave us the inheritance of the kingdom of God, and thus, delivered us from the opposite outcome, which would be wrath.

Chapter 1 Questions

1. What is the main function of the pastor?

2. What makes the heart of the pastor rejoice?

3. What is the motivation of the believer?

4. How should we preach the gospel?

5. How should we receive the gospel?

6. What is the truth that encourages us to receive the gospel of Christ with endurance?

2

Chapter Outline

• The proper attitude of the servant (1-12)
• The fruits of his ministry (13-16)
• St. Paul's concern for them (17-20)

Introduction

The believers in Thessalonica were going through a difficult time because of persecution. That is why they needed a word of comfort and encouragement. In this chapter, St. Paul encourages them to endure persecution by emphasizing his love and fatherhood to them. Also, he praised them for accepting the word of God as not just being the word of men, but truly of God. He also praised them for enduring persecution with perseverance. He concludes the chapter by explaining his longing to see them and why he could not visit them earlier.

This is one of the most important chapters in the entire Bible related to service and ministry. I hope that every servant reads this chapter repeatedly and learns from the principles that St. Paul mentioned here in order to have a successful ministry

.

2:1-12 In this set of verses, you will learn about the proper attributes of a true servant: (1) We need to serve with courage and boldness; (2) We need to preach the gospel in truth, holiness, and love; (3) We must seek the glory of God, and not our own glory; (4) We must seek to please God, and not to be men-pleasers; (5) We must conduct ourselves with gentleness, (6) sacrificial love, (7) devotedness, justness, and blamelessness; (8) We must exhort, charge, and comfort people; (9) This should all be done in the spirit of fatherhood, and also like a nursing mother; (10) The goal of service is clear: to help situate a people that walk worthy of God's kingdom and glory..

2:1 For you, yourselves, know, brethren, that our coming to you was not in vain. St. Paul here is speaking about the fruit of his ministry. The ministry of the apostles to the Thessalonians *"was not in vain"* because it brought forth fruits. The endurance of persecution itself is one of the fruits of the faithful ministry of St. Paul. Add to that also, the Thessalonians' belief that the gospel is not simply the word of men, but actually the word of God (see 2:13 below). St. Paul does not want them to say the ministry of St. Paul and the apostles is failing; instead, it should be viewed as not being "in vain," having brought forth fruits.

2:2 But even after we had suffered before and were spitefully treated at Philippi, as you know, we were bold in our God to speak to you the gospel of God in much conflict. St. Paul is telling them, "You know that we suffered in Philippi" (which suffering, you can read about it in Acts 16). This suffering did not stop the apostles from preaching to the Thessalonians in order to avoid more suffering, but actually after having suffered, they were *"bold"* in God to speak the gospel of God in the midst of much conflict. ✤ We must have such boldness to speak the gospel of God even if there is suffering and hardship around us. Our boldness comes from God (as St. Paul says, *"we were bold in our God."*). He will give us courage in order to be able to speak and preach the gospel of Christ irrespective of the conflicts we confront.

2:3 For our exhortation did not come from error or uncleanness, nor was it in deceit. Suffering (such as that experienced by the Thessalonians) is not an indication that there is an error of the apostles' message, but rather can signify that the message is true, being attacked by Satan.

error. "Error" here refers to teachings such as that of the Gnostics or Judaizers. For example, Christians who were formerly Jewish were teaching that Christians must keep the law of the Old Testament (e.g., circumcision, purification, sacrifices) in order to be saved; Gnosticism exalted knowledge above faith. St. Paul, however, clarifies that the Christian message proclaimed by the apostles was not in error..

uncleanness. The message of the apostles was not like the pagans, who often utilized a plethora of varied impure actions and rituals in their worship. The gospel of Christ, however, is filled with holiness.

nor was it in deceit. Deceit refers to the erroneous idea that the message of the apostles was meant to deceive people, as if there was some second or hidden agenda underlying it (such as St. Paul seeking popularity, glory, or greed). On the contrary, this message is of truth (not error), holiness (not uncleanness), and genuine love (not deceit). We can say that these three elements are essential elements in preaching the gospel.

✤ *Four attributes of a servant ~* We should preach in boldness (v.2), declaring the truth (v.3), which is holy (v.3), and relayed out of love (v.3).

2:4 But as we have been approved by God to be entrusted with the gospel, even so we speak, not as pleasing men, but God who tests our hearts. Another criterion of a proper servant is presented here: are you men pleasers or do you desire to please God.

Many people in their service seek to please men rather than God. St. Paul indicates that this was not the heart by which he and the apostles preach, for it is God who tests their hearts. Thus, the goal is not to please men but rather God. When God examined the hearts of the apostles, they were *"approved by God to be entrusted with the gospel."* He found their hearts after His own heart (cf., 1 Sam. 13:14). ✤ Servants should ask themselves, "When God examines my heart, does He approve me to be entrusted with preaching the gospel or not?"

2:5 **For neither at any time did we use flattering words, as you know, nor a cloak for covetousness— God is witness.** St. Paul elaborates more here about why he was not a men pleaser. Usually, such people use flattering words to please men. St. Paul also did not have the ulterior motive of covetousness, being greedy to make profit out of his service. Usually, the covetous person uses deceit in order to reach his goals; however, St. Paul already indicated that he did not preach in a manner of *"deceit"* (v.3). St. Paul does not seek approval from the people, but rather, it is God who examines the hearts and tests hearts (v.4), who is a witness that what St. Paul preaches is true.

2:6 **Nor did we seek glory from men, either from you or from others, when we might have made demands as apostles of Christ.** St. Paul expresses another attribute of a good servant (similar to the one previously expressed): seeking the glory of God, not their own glory from men. As apostles of Christ, they could have used their authority to glorify themselves or to fulfill their demands or needs. This was never the case, however, refusing even the demands and honor due them as being apostles of Christ. ✤ St. Paul is setting for us a very important principle. Authority in service is given to serve others, not to rule, control, or demand others.

2:7 **But we were gentle among you, just as a nursing mother cherishes her own children.** St. Paul focuses on the manner in which the apostles preached to the Thessalonians. He describes their preaching as being *"gentle."* The servant should be like a nursing mother, full of compassion and affection. This should be the heart of the servant. And if you think about the nursing mother, she does not expect any glory, money, or fulfillment of her demands in return for caring for her child. This should be the heart of the servant.

2:8 So, affectionately longing for you, we were well pleased to impart to you not only the gospel of God, but also our own lives, because you had become dear to us. As a nursing mother (v.7; see also 1 Kings 3:16-27) is willing to die for her children (sacrificial love), St. Paul declares that the apostles are willing to sacrifice their own lives for the Thessalonians. This is a very strong message, one which Christ said of Himself: *"As the Father knows Me, even so I know the Father; and I lay down My life for the sheep"* (John 10:15). The servant's heart should be full of love for his people. This love should be unconditional for those whom he serves, regardless of their status or spirituality, as the love of Christ is toward us: *"But God demonstrates His own love toward us, in that while we were still sinners, Christ died for us"* (Rom. 5:8). This love must also be sacrificial and limitless (not limited to a certain group, but for everyone).

2:9 For you remember, brethren, our labor and toil; for laboring night and day, that we might not be a burden to any of you, we preached to you the gospel of God. The love of the apostles was not only in words, but was translated in action as well. The manner by which St. Paul sacrificed his life for his flock included a desire not to burden them with his financial needs; that is why, besides preaching the gospel, he and the apostles worked day and night to provide for their needs. Although God provided a principal—that servants of the altar, from the altar should eat, nonetheless, St. Paul and the apostles did not take advantage of this right, demonstrating their sacrificial love by not burdening the people to minister to the apostles' needs.

2:10 You are witnesses, and God also, how devoutly and justly and blamelessly we behaved ourselves among you who believe. There are three more criteria mentioned here regarding the proper attitude of a servant: devoutness, justice, and blamelessness. If servants keep these three principles, they will have a very successful ministry.

You are witnesses. God is not the only witness (v.4) of the apostles, but so too are those whom they serve who can testify as to how they behaved among the people.

devoutly. Preaching the ministry took priority in his life.

justly. St. Paul treated everyone with fairness, showing no partiality in his ministry (cf., James 2:9, 3:17).

blamelessly. St. Paul strove not to offend anyone.

2:11   as you know how we exhorted, and comforted, and charged every one of you, as a father does his own children. St. Paul's preaching was in the spirit of fatherhood. As a servant, he understood his ministry to exhort, comfort, and charge, yet as a father speaking to his children whom he loves.

exhorted. This is to motivate people to live a life of holiness and repentance.

comforted. When a person falls in their repentance, or if there are obstacles in their life as they strive to be holy, the servant should encourage and motivate with a message of hope to help them rise again (see Micah 7:7-8).

charged. This is to provide practical means to apply the lessons regarding how to live a life of holiness and repentance.

2:12 that you would walk worthy of God who calls you into His own kingdom and glory. St. Paul knows the goal of his ministry: to help all people to be blameless and holy before God in His Second Coming. Think of a prince who marries a poor girl from a poor family. When she marries into the royal family, she should conduct herself in a manner befitting of being a part of her new royal family. That is what St. Paul is saying now. Now that you are the children of God and have been called to His kingdom: *"But you are a chosen generation, a royal priesthood, a holy nation, His own special people, that you may proclaim the praises of Him who called you out of darkness into His marvelous light"* (1 Pet. 2:9). You need to walk worthy of this calling and of God who called you into His kingdom and His glory.

2:13-16 In the beginning of this chapter, St. Paul told the Thessalonians, *"you yourselves know, brethren, that our coming to you was not in vain"* (v.1). From verses 13-16, St. Paul explains to them the fruits of his ministry among them. These fruits actually were due to the work of the Holy Spirit. If God did not work with St. Paul, these fruits would not have been achievable. That is why, before discussing the fruits of his ministry, St. Paul says, *"we also thank God without ceasing"* (v.13). When we find our ministry successful and fruitful, we should not boast in ourselves, but give thanks to God who is the source of every victory, success, and triumph (cf., 2 Cor. 2:14).

2:13   For this reason we also thank God without ceasing, because when you received the word of God which you heard from us. When St. Paul preached to the Thessalonians, they did not accept his words as simply words of men, but instead, as words of

God.

you welcomed it not as the word of men, but as it is in truth, the word of God. Think of this phrase: "as it is in truth, the word of God." The preaching of St. Paul and the apostles is not their own preaching, but it is the word of God which they are spreading. This is very important to know and understand in our current time. His Holiness Pope Shenouda III tells a story about when he was speaking with the Episcopal Church about the ordination of homosexuals. He was speaking to them from the letters of St. Paul which clearly indicate that homosexuality is a sin. A person responded to His Holiness and said, "But these are the words of St. Paul, not the words of Christ." This was very sad because they differentiate between what is attributed to Christ's own preaching during His ministry, and the writings written by His followers. This was said although we know that every word in *"all Scripture is given by inspiration of God"* (2 Tim. 3:16), whether that be of the Old or of the New Testament (cf., 2 Peter 3:15-16 where St. Peter puts St. Paul's letters on the same footing as the Old Testament, and also 1 Timothy 5:18 where St. Paul quotes from a passage found in Deuteronomy followed by a statement of our Lord found in the Gospel according to St. Luke. St. Paul was affirming that his gospel was not the words of men, but the words of God: *"as it is in truth, the word of God."* The fact that the Thessalonians accepted this principle, that the preaching of St. Paul was the gospel of truth and not simply the words of mere men, this displayed the first fruit of the apostles' ministry.

which also effectively works in you who believe. Since St. Paul's message was the word of God and not of men, then it was working effectively in the Thessalonians. The word of God has power in itself. Here, let us understand the principle of inspiration of Scripture (the word of God). The Holy Spirit did not simply inspire the writers in the Bible to write what they wrote and then just left everything alone. Rather, until now, every time we hear the word of God or preach it, the Holy Spirit accompanies every word in the Bible. When we receive it, we do so by the power in every word. That is why St. Paul in Hebrews said, *"For the word of God is living and powerful, and sharper than any two-edged sword, piercing even to the division of soul and spirit, and of joints and marrow, and is a discerner of the thoughts and intents of the heart"* (Heb. 4:12). The Holy Spirit can effectively work in us who believe. That is what happened with the Thessalonians. When they heard the word of God, they were transformed so that they would be able to endure suffering and persecution with courage and motivation. When we receive the word of God as truly His word, it will transform us and work effectively in us.

2:14 **For you, brethren, became imitators of the churches of God which are in Judea in Christ Jesus. For you also suffered the same things from your own countrymen, just as they did from the Judeans.** The Thessalonians are being commended here because other churches in Judea are beginning to imitate them in their endurance of persecution which they were facing from Jewish people in Jerusalem. This endurance is another fruit of the ministry to the Thessalonians. This is not strange, as Christ Himself endured pain from the Jewish people, and the church in Jerusalem endured also much suffering by the Jews; thus, it should not be considered a strange thing that the Thessalonians are enduring suffering from their own countrymen. This is expected that those who want to live according to the gospel of Christ. (*"These things I have spoken to you, that in Me you may have peace. In the world you will have tribulation; but be of good cheer, I have overcome the world."*—John 16:33).

2:15 Here and in the next verse, we hear about the sins of the Jews.

who killed both the Lord Jesus and their own prophets, and have persecuted us. The Judeans killed Christ and also, when God sent them prophets (like Isaiah or Jeremiah), they killed them too. They also persecuted the apostles and the Christians.

and they do not please God and are contrary to all men. St. Paul said this because he himself was a Jew, bearing much indignation and prejudice against the Christians (*"Indeed, I myself thought I must do many things contrary to the name of Jesus of Nazareth."*— Acts 26:9; *"They will put you out of the synagogues; yes, the time is coming that whoever kills you will think that he offers God service."*— John 16:2). Although the Jews believe that they are pleasing God by killing and opposing Christians, they are not. They began to be *"contrary to all men"* as Christianity began to spread everywhere.

2:16 **forbidding us to speak to the Gentiles that they may be saved.** It is even the case that many of the Jews who believed in the Lord Christ became Christians and were opposed to the apostles' preaching to the Gentiles, thinking that heaven was only made for the Jewish people. They do not want anyone to be saved except the Judeans only. Maybe that was the problem of Jonah when he did not want to preach to Nineveh, not desiring that Gentiles be saved.

so as always to fill up the measure of their sins; but wrath has come upon them to the uttermost. By all the sins mentioned previously (killing Christ and the prophets, persecuting

Christians, forbidding the apostles from preaching, causing great displeasure to God, and being contrary to men), the Jews have filled up the measure of their sins. Thus, St. Paul says they are deserving of the "uttermost" wrath. This letter was written about 52 A.D. It is believed that St. Paul was here prophetically declaring the destruction of Jerusalem, which happened about 18 years later (70 A.D.). Their temple was destroyed and they were scattered all over the world. (Note that it is said that the Roman leader of the siege of Jerusalem which led to the destruction of the Temple, Titus, reportedly refused to accept a wreath of victory, saying that the victory did not come through his own efforts but that he had merely served as an instrument of God's wrath.—Philostratus, The Life of Apollonius of Tyana, 6:29).

2:17-20   St. Paul discusses his concern for them and that he was hindered by Satan from visiting them. This teaches us that many times Satan can hinder us from achieving our goals. He even hindered Archangel Gabriel from delivering a message to Daniel the Prophet (for 21 days—Daniel 10:13). But, this should not scare us; instead, it should motivate us to pray, for if God is with us, no one can be against us: *"What then shall we say to these things? If God is for us, who can be against us?"* (Rom. 8:31).

2:17   **But we, brethren, having been taken away from you for a short time in presence, not in heart.** I like what St. Paul says here. You can read about how St. Paul was forced to leave Thessalonica in Acts 17:1-9. When he left, he indicated that he was *"taken away"* from them but only in presence. The spiritual bond among the apostles and the Thessalonians was beyond time and place. Although physically absent, their hearts remained bonded to them.

endeavored more eagerly to see your face with great desire. Having been taken away from the Thessalonians, the apostles remained longing with great desire to see their face.

✠   *Genuine motivation for servant visitations* ~ Here is another principle being set by St. Paul that can be applied to the servants. The motivation behind visitation (when a priest or a servant makes a personal visit to their people whom they serve) should be love and longing to be with them, not just to calm one's conscience, out of guilt, or out of routine. It should be done with eagerness and great desire.

2:18   **Therefore we wanted to come to you—even I, Paul.** Not only did the apostles want to go and visit the Thessalonians, but St. Paul makes it clear that he himself desired the same.

time and again—but Satan hindered us. This refers to the persecution which prevented them from returning to the Thessalonians.

2:19-20 **For what is our hope, or joy, or crown of rejoicing? Is it not even you in the presence of our Lord Jesus Christ at His coming? For you are our glory and joy.** St. Paul now addresses the question, "What is the reason for our love to you? What is the reason for our eagerness and desire for you?" St. Paul is imagining himself standing before God at the last day. He is telling God, here I am with all my people and churches which I have established, and all who have believed in you because of my ministry. These people will be St. Paul's hope in the last day for victory over Satan, taking all these people from the kingdom of Satan and translating them to the kingdom of God. They are his hope and joy when he sees all of them saved with him and inheriting heaven. This will be the crown that brings joy to his heart.

✠ *Those whom you serve are not to be regarded as a burden or a "cross"* ~ Unfortunately, many of the clergy and servants think of their people whom they serve as a burden or a cross, but St. Paul actually had a very joyful perception of them. He saw the people as a *"hope"* and *"joy"* and *"crown of rejoicing"*: *"For you are our glory and joy."* This is true. Because of ministry

and service, we will be qualified to be crowned, to be joyful in the time of Christ, and to have hope. I want every servant and priest to think of their people and flock as their *"crown of rejoicing"* and *"glory and joy."* This is a very important principle. .

Chapter 2 Questions

1. What had St. Paul endured prior to coming to Thessalonica?

2. What was his attitude when he arrived?

3. How should a servant conduct himself in his ministry?

4. What is the function of authority in service?

5. What is the indication that we accept the word of God as truly His word and not just the word of men?

6. What should be the motive of servant visitations?

7. Who will be our hope, glory, joy, and crown of rejoicing in the Second Coming of the Lord?

3

Chapter Outline

- Timothy's visit (1-5)
- Timothy's report (6-11)
- St. Paul's prayer (12-13)

3:1-2 Therefore, when we could no longer endure it, we thought it good to be left in Athens alone, and sent Timothy. St. Paul is telling the Thessalonians, "When we received the news of your persecution, we could no longer endure not knowing more about your condition, and not being with them in their difficult time supporting, establishing, and encouraging them in the faith." St. Paul tried to visit a number of times, but Satan hindered him (1 Thess. 2:18). So, he sent St. Timothy for two reasons: (1) to assess their faith, seeing if they had been shaken by the tribulations they faced (v.5 below); and (2) to encourage the Thessalonians concerning their faith.

Timothy, our brother and minister of God, and our fellow laborer in the gospel of Christ, to establish you and encourage you concerning your faith. What does it mean that St. Timothy was sent to them? St. Timothy was a disciple of St. Paul, which means that upon him, St. Paul relied a lot. By leaving St. Paul's side,

St. Paul was being left alone in Athens without the support of St. Timothy. The description of St. Timothy as being a *"brother and minister of God, and our fellow laborer in the gospel of Christ"* shows how humble St. Paul was. Although St. Timothy was in actuality a spiritual son of St. Paul (see 1 Tim. 1:1), who was ordained as a bishop by him (1 Tim. 1:2-3 and 2 Tim. 1:6), St. Paul calls him a *"brother"* and *"fellow laborer."* By indicating in verse 1 that the apostles *"thought it good to be left alone in Athens,"* we can understand St. Paul as saying, "Timothy is a great support to me, but in spite of my need for him, I will choose to remain without him in Athens and send him to you (Thessalonians) because of my love for you and my desire that he establish you and encourage you." Thus, this all reflects St. Paul's humility as well as his love for St. Timothy and towards the Thessalonians (putting them before his own personal needs, heeding his own advice to the Corinthians that *"love ... does not seek its own"* (1 Cor. 13:4-5).

❊ *"Salvation in a moment" theology contravened in this verse* ~ - Some denominations of Christianity teach that once a person is saved, he or she is always saved and that no believer can perish. However, if this doctrine was true, then why was St. Paul concerned about the Thessalonians? They believed and accepted salvation. The doctrine of "once saved, always saved" is simply not true.

3:3-5 In these verses St. Paul is giving us some important teachings and facts about suffering from which we can extract seven points:

(1) During the time of suffering, the faith of many can be shaken.

(2) Satan can use the time of suffering to cast doubt in our hearts.

(3) Suffering may challenge the work and ministry of the servants.

(4) We should expect suffering and not consider it a strange thing.

(5) The Church should prepare the children for suffering, because this is a requirement of discipleship to the Lord.

(6) During the time of suffering, we should be concerned about one another and support each other.

(7) The Church has a responsibility to support and help people during their times of suffering.

3:3 **that no one should be shaken by these afflictions.** Suffering can shake our faith, which is evident by the many people whose faith or reliance on God dwindles when they go through a hard time. Although when we speak about persecution, we often focus on the martyrs and how they confessed their faith, by the same token, many people who faced persecution converted to other religions and denied Christ because they could not endure

the suffering.

for you yourselves know that we are appointed to this. We should expect suffering. It is not a strange thing when we find ourselves confronted with tribulation. "We are appointed to this." Many people are surprised when there is persecution or hardship against the church, and they wonder why this happened. Many people, unfortunately, believe that good people should not suffer, questioning all the time why bad things happen to good people. On the contrary, the teaching of the Bible is that bad things will happen to good people. If good people should not suffer, then the Lord Jesus Christ should not have suffered since he is the Holy One and without sin. However, the Lord Jesus Christ is our pioneer in suffering and carrying the cross.

3:4 **For, in fact, we told you before when we were with you that we would suffer tribulation, just as it happened, and you know.** The Church should prepare people to endure suffering they will face. This is part of the message the Church should deliver. The Lord Christ Himself said, *"Whoever desires to come after Me, let him deny himself, and take up his cross, and follow Me"* (Mark 8:34). There is no Christianity without a cross. *"Yes, and all who desire to live godly in Christ Jesus will suffer persecution"* (2 Tim. 3:12). I say this because many preachers nowadays want to present Christianity without suffering or a cross, to make it just a "feel-good" religion. This is not the teaching of the Bible. St. Paul taught the flock in the church of the Thessalonians that suffering would come and tried to prepare them for it.

3:5   For this reason, when I could no longer endure it, I sent to know your faith. This teaches us that during the time of suffering, we should be concerned about one another and support each other. During suffering, the faith of people may be shaken and Satan may take advantage of people's weaknesses during this time. Thus, we must be concerned about one another. If we see one of our brethren suffering, we must support and surround that person until the time of suffering passes. This is not only the responsibility of one another but also the responsibility of the church, to support people as they face tribulation. That is why St. Paul sent St. Timothy to encourage and help the Thessalonians during the spiritual turbulence they were facing. ✠ As a father, St. Paul could not endure knowing that the Thessalonians were suffering. He mentions the notion of not being able to *"endure"* it any longer twice (v.1 and v.5)

lest by some means the tempter had tempted you. Suffering can be a good opportunity for Satan to tempt us, as said in verse 5: *"lest by some means*

the tempter had tempted you, and our labor might be in vain." Usually, Satan takes advantage of suffering and tries to convince us that God doesn't love us or care about us. Often times, people who are in the midst of tribulation are convinced to blame God for what they are going through, saying such things as, "Why did God let this happen? Why did God allow this? Where is God? If God really loves us, where is He?" That is what Satan does, casting doubt on our faith in God and His promises.

and our labor might be in vain. Suffering can cause the labor of the servants to be *"in vain."* The clergy and servants may work very hard to encourage the people to confirm them in their faith, yet because of suffering and its effect on people, their labor will be *"in vain"* in the sense that it does not bear the expected fruits. Satan challenges the work of the ministry. That is why in many countries which used to be predominantly Christian, during the time of persecution, we find that many of them denied Christianity and converted to other religions. ✠ St. Paul wanted to relay to the Thessalonians the idea that their success is his success, and their failure is his failure, as he said in the previous chapter (*"For what is our hope, or joy, or crown of rejoicing? Is it not even you in the presence of our Lord Jesus Christ at His coming? For you are our glory and joy."*—1 Thess. 2:19-20). When St. Paul sent St. Timothy rather than going himself, some people began to doubt St. Paul's genuineness in caring about the people of Thessalonica. St. Paul tells them that he cares about them, but Satan hindered him. They should not think St. Paul does not care because if they are shaken by suffering it means his ministry was in vain: *"Your success is my success, and your failure is my failure."* St. Paul was absolutely invested in the wellbeing of the church in Thessalonica. Also, to have sent St. Timothy, who is not just any servant but a spiritual son who is regarded as a *"fellow laborer"* of St. Paul's (v.2 above), this further indicates the overwhelming love and care for the Thessalonians

3:6-11 St. Paul speaks about St. Timothy's report when he came back from Thessalonica. In v.6 we read about what St. Timothy's report was, and beginning in v.7 St. Paul responds to the report from St. Timothy.

3:6 But now that Timothy has come to us from you, and brought us good news of your faith and love, and that you always have good remembrance of us, greatly desiring to see us, as we also to see you. The report of St. Timothy included three elements: (1) How their love and faith is strong and was not shaken by persecution and suffering; (2) Continued remembrance of St. Paul in a positive way, speaking well of St. Paul and his companions; (3) Their desire to see St. Paul in the future, which St. Paul

clarifies is a mutual longing and can be summed up as follows: "As you desire to see us, so we also desire to see you."

3:7 therefore, brethren, in all our affliction and distress we were comforted concerning you by your faith. He felt comforted and joyful amidst his affliction which he was facing in Athens. ✤ It brings joy, peace, and comfort to the heart of a spiritual father to see his children abiding in Christ and growing in the grace of God. Many times, we only share our problems and bad news with our spiritual fathers, but when we also share good news with them, it is a source of joy and comfort even in the midst of affliction and distress through which they endure.

3:8 For now we live, if you stand fast in the Lord. St. Paul reacts to the report about the Thessalonians also by expressing that they are, in a sense, his life: if their faith is shaken, St. Paul feels as if he is dying, and if their faith is strong, it is as if he is really living, although he may be suffering from various afflictions.

3:9 For what thanks can we render to God for you, for all the joy with which we rejoice for your sake before our God. St. Paul did not give any credit to himself for the spiritual wellbeing of the Thessalonians. Instead of claiming his own steadfastness in the ministry as the reason for their strong faith, St. Paul knew that if there is any success in the service to God, it is from God. Thus, he opened his heart saying, *"what thanks can we render to God for you?"* Many times when our ministry succeeds, we give credit to ourselves (even if we do not admit it or say it, or are aware that we are feeling it, it happens in our hearts). St. Paul said, though, that he is nothing, and that he renders thanks to God for the fruit of the ministry, as he told the Ephesians: *"I became a minister according to the gift of the grace of God given to me by the effective working of His power"* (Eph. 3:7); and to the Corinthians he writes: *"But by the grace of God I am what I am, and His grace toward me was not in vain; but I labored more abundantly than they all, yet not I, but the grace of God which was with me"* (1 Cor. 15:10), as well as, *"According to the grace of God which was given to me, as a wise master builder I have laid the foundation, and another builds on it. But let each one take heed how he builds on it"* (1 Cor. 3:10). When we hear good news about our flock, the first thing we should do is to give thanks to God that this ministry is succeeding.

3:10 night and day praying exceedingly that we may see your face and perfect what is lacking in your faith? Aside from giving thanks to God, St. Paul continued to pray *"exceedingly"* without ceasing (*"night and day"*), hoping that God would ease the way to see the Thessalonians and support them in what is lacking in their faith.

perfect what is lacking in your faith? St. Timothy reported *"good news"* of their *"faith and love,"* (v.6) so then, what is lacking. I do not think St. Paul was speaking about their faith in terms of it being a virtue of strong belief in God, but rather referring to the doctrine of their faith. It is possible St. Paul did not have a chance to teach the Thessalonians about the concept of death in Christianity and what happens after death. This would explain why in the next chapter St. Paul diverts his attention to speaking about those who die in Christ and the Second Coming of the Lord Jesus Christ. St. Paul, then, was praying to see the Thessalonians in particular to teach them about matters of doctrine that he had not previously taught them, maybe from lack of time.

3:11 Now may our God and Father Himself, and our Lord Jesus Christ, direct our way to you. This shows that, although *"Satan hindered"* (1 Thess. 2:18) St. Paul and the apostles from seeing the Thessalonians, St. Paul, nonetheless, believed that God can direct his way to them. He knows that everything that is done is by the will or permission of God. When it is God's will for St. Paul to visit the Thessalonians, he is sure God will remove all the obstacles that stand in his way. ✠ St. Paul's feelings with regard to the Holy Trinity were very strong. Usually (as can be seen in many letters), he freely speaks about the Father, the Son, and the Holy Spirit. He was always interacting with the three hypostases of the Holy Trinity. Here, he appealed to the Father and to the Son, to direct His way to the Thessalonians.

3:12-13 St. Paul concludes this chapter by a prayer for the Thessalonians, which consists of two parts: (1) praying for their spiritual growth; and (2) praying that at the time of the Second Coming of our Lord Jesus Christ, they would be without blame.

3:12 And may the Lord make you increase and abound in love to one another. St. Paul prays that the Thessalonians *"increase and abound in love."* This growth cannot occur without God, as the Lord Jesus Christ said, *"without Me you can do nothing"* (John 15:5). That is why St. Paul implores God for the growth he is seeking for the Thessalonians. If you want to grow in your spiritual life, then you need to learn the life of prayer, without which you cannot grow.

love. The main focus of growth which St. Paul prays for is love. We can summarize the entire Bible in one word: love. If you think about *"which is the great commandment in the law"* (Matt. 22:36), for example, the Lord God summarized everything in two commandments: *"Jesus said to him, 'You shall love the Lord your God with all your heart, with all your soul, and with all your mind.' This is the first and great commandment. And the second is like it: 'You shall love your neighbor as yourself'"* (Matt. 22:37-39). That is what all of Christianity is. That is why love is the primary virtue sought for spiritual growth. ✠ Although St. Timothy brought good news about their faith and love (v.6), to the extent that St. Paul will mention in the next chapter that *"concerning brotherly love,"* he has *"no need"* to write to them (1 Thess. 4:9). Nonetheless, St. Paul encourages them to increase in love because there is always room to grow: *"But concerning brotherly love you have no need that I should write to you, for you yourselves are taught by God to love one another; and indeed you do so toward all the brethren who are in all Macedonia. But we urge you, brethren, that you increase more and more"* (1 Thess. 4:9-10). God is infinite, and *"God is love"* (1 John 4:8). Thus, no one can claim to have reached perfection in love. Everyone needs to pray and seek to increase in this virtue. ✠ Love is needed all the time, but is most needed during the time of hardship and suffering, through which we can stand fast and face tribulation without having our faith shaken

and to all, just as we do to you. Love is meant not only for our brethren in the church, but everyone else, including our enemies. That is true love and the Christian standard by which we should abide. St. Paul provides them the example of himself (and other apostles) who put the Thessalonians first before his own personal needs.

3:13 **so that He may establish your hearts blameless in holiness before our God and Father at the coming of our Lord Jesus Christ with all His saints.** St. Paul makes clear that the Lord Jesus Christ will come again to judge the Thessalonians (and everyone else), and that He will come again with the saints. The term *"saints"* here includes both angels and righteous people. It is very important for us, in the second coming of Christ, to be holy and without blame. When we grow in love, our hearts will be established *"blameless in holiness."* Then, when the Lord appears in His Second Coming, we will not be judged with blame. We need to grow in love. Love purifies our hearts. Love teaches us to be without blame. When I love my brother, I will not hurt him, and even if there is a conflict between us, I will ask for forgiveness, seeking reconciliation. This is as St. Augustine

said, *"Love God and do as you please."* When we truly love God, we will never disappoint Him, whereby, we can be established without blame and appear in holiness before our Lord Jesus Christ. ✤ St. Paul concludes with this verse about the Second Coming of our Lord Jesus Christ to introduce the upcoming discussion in the following chapter.

Chapter 3 Questions

1. Why did St. Paul send Timothy?

2. What can happen to believers because of suffering?

3. What is the church role regarding suffering?

4. What is the church role regarding suffering?

5. How can we become a source of joy and comfort to our spiritual fathers?

6. For what did St. Paul pray concerning the Thessalonians?

7. What do we need to be blameless in the last day?

4

Chapter Outline

- Walking in holiness (1-7)
- Walk in love (9-10)
- Walk in diligence (11-12)
- Walk in hope (13-18)

Introduction

St. Paul concluded the previous chapter by saying, *"so that He may establish your hearts blameless in holiness before our God and Father at the coming of our Lord Jesus Christ with all His saints"* (1 Thess. 3:13). He was praying that the Lord may establish their hearts blameless and in holiness in the Second Coming of our Lord Christ. This is a very important and good prayer that we all need so that with holy and blameless hearts, we may go with the Lord joyfully to the kingdom of Heaven. In this chapter, St. Paul instructs the Thessalonians regarding their role of being blameless when the Lord returns for His Second Coming. He will discuss four points: Walking in holiness, love, diligence, and hope.

4:1 Finally then, brethren, we urge and exhort in the Lord Jesus. St. Paul is urging and exhorting them in the Lord Jesus. What does he mean by saying, *"in the Lord Jesus"*? This means that St. Paul is speaking as an apostle by the authority of God, whereby his words are not of himself but are the words of God. Thus, the exhortation he is about to proclaim is from God and not from St. Paul. Moreover, speaking *"in the Lord Jesus"* refers to the notion that St. Paul speaks with the power of the Lord Jesus Christ, who gives St. Paul the authority to be His apostle.

that you should abound more and more. We should always grow in what we hear and in what we receive from our spiritual fathers. Through the teachings which we receive or that we read, or the instructions that we learn, we should abound in them more and more. The sign of life is growth. If you have a plant that is not growing, it means it is dead; if it is growing, we know it is alive. Thus, in our lives, we need to grow every day in the commandments and teachings that we receive.

just as you received from us. This reflects the spirit of discipleship. The believers are disciples of their spiritual fathers, being disciplined by them and learning from them, receiving the teachings of the Holy Spirit from them. This also refers to the apostolic traditions that were received from the apostles and have been diligently kept until today.

how you ought to walk and to please God. We need to *"walk worthy of the calling with which we were called"* (Eph. 4:1). We are called to be separate from people and from the world. We are called to be in His likeness and image. We are called to live according to His holy commandments and by the grace of God. We cannot please God unless we walk according to His commandments (see also Rom. 8:8; 2 Tim. 2:4; Heb. 11:6).

4:2   for you know what commandments we gave you through the Lord Jesus. *"Through the Lord Jesus"* means (as in the last verse), "through the power of the Lord Jesus" and by the authority received from God and given to the apostles. The commandments the apostles deliver to the people are not their own, but they relay what they have received from God.

✤ *Do we pay attention to God's words and commandments?* ~ As listeners and disciples, we must pay attention to these commandments because these are words of God. Many people do not pay attention to the teachings. You may attend, for example, the service of the Liturgy, and after the Liturgy if someone asks you about the readings, it will be obvious you were not paying attention. However, here, St. Paul tells the Thessalonians, *"you know what commandments we gave you."* Do we know what commandments are given to us every day, in every Liturgy, and every spiritual gathering which we attend in church? As believers and

disciples, we should be attentive to all the commandments we hear and take them seriously, growing and abounding more and more (cf., v.1).

4:3   For this is the will of God, your sanctification. Many people ask, "What is the will of God in my life?" St. Paul summarizes the answer for us in one simple phrase: *"your sanctification."* If you are facing a decision in life and are not sure which way to go, ask yourself, "Is this conducive to my sanctification, or not? Will this help me be holy or not?"

sanctification. Sanctification means to be separate from the rest of the world. The word *"holy"* means to separate. When we say we consecrate a church, for example, we are saying that this church is being set apart (separated) from the rest of the world and being dedicated completely to God. If you are sanctified to God, this means you are dedicated to Him, being separate from the rest of the world, living a holy life (one with no sin—cf., Luke 1:6). Sanctification is a broad term, and in the verses below, he will whittle this word down to more specific aspects to address the goal of sanctification of our entire beings.

that you should abstain from sexual immorality. Although St. Paul was speaking in general about every sin (sanctification), he emphasized, in particular, the importance of living in purity. It is very important to live a holy and godly life, as St. Paul says to the Hebrews: *"holiness, without which no one will see the Lord"* (Heb. 12:14). St. Paul now is focusing on one point: to abstain from sexual immorality in all its forms. Why? Because God cannot dwell in a heart that is not pure. Sexual immorality defiles our heart and makes it unsuitable for the dwelling of God. We read in the Beatitudes, *"Blessed are the pure in heart, for they shall see God"* (Matt. 5:8). In order to be able to see God and for Him to dwell in your heart, you must be pure and abstain from all forms of sexual immorality. .

4:4   that each of you should know how to possess his own vessel in sanctification and honor.   St. Paul further narrows the notion of sanctification by abstinence from sexual immorality, describing specifically the notion of each of us possessing our own vessel in sanctification and honor.

his own vessel. The Church interprets this word as either referring to one's own body or one's spouse. In actuality, there is no difference to both interpretations since in marriage the two become one flesh. Thus, after marriage your body and the body of your spouse are one— your body.

4:5   not in passion of lust, like the Gentiles who do not know God. Your body is the temple of God, like the Church, consecrated by the Holy Chrism (or Myron), just like we concentrate the holy vessels of the altar and the altar itself. St. Paul said in his first letter to the Corinthians, *"Do you not know that your body is the temple of the Holy Spirit who is in you, whom you have from God, and you are not your own?"* (1 Cor. 6:19). You need to respect your body and possess it in sanctification and honor. Do not despise your body or defile it. A person who does not keep the purity of his body is doing just that: defiling and despising the temple of God, which is your body.

✤ *Proper intimacy between husband and wife* ~ we can understand this verse as reflecting a lesson about the intimate relationship between husband and wife. How does a spouse "possess his own vessel in sanctification and honor, not in passion of lust, like the Gentiles who do not know God." Unfortunately, nonbelievers and those who are not truly Christian accept some practices in the intimate relationship between husband and wife as being normal, when they are not. Many practices are abnormal and displeasing to God. Thus, St. Paul tells us here about such practices, "We, as children of God, know Him and in our relationship we must possess one another in sanctification and honor." St. Paul tells us in Hebrews, "Marriage is honorable among all, and the bed undefiled; but fornicators and adulterers

God will judge" (Heb. 13:4). Many wonder how the bed of marriage can be defiled. Not all the forms of intimate practices which the world introduces to us are acceptable or godly. You should not imitate the Gentiles who do not know God in such practices, but rather possess your body (your spouse and yourself) in sanctification and honor.

not ... like the Gentiles. St. Paul gave many reasons for why we should not walk *"in passion of lust, like the Gentiles who do not know God."* (1) He said that our Christian bodies are not like those of the Gentiles who do not know God, for our bodies are temples of the Holy Spirit. The nonbelievers do not have the Holy Spirit dwelling in them. We, Christians, receive the Holy Spirit in the Mystery of Chrismation. (2) You know God, but they do not know Him. Knowing God means you have the grace of God in your heart and are walking in His fear. Thus, you should possess your vessel in sanctification and honor. The knowledge of God is life and it gives grace and power, purifying your heart and sanctifying your body. (3) We, as Christians, love each other as expressed by the Greek term for love (of which there are many), which is "Agape," rather that "Eros." Eros is lustful love which receives only and is selfish. Agape is unconditional and giving all the time, always being sacrificial (see 1 Cor. 13). The love between the husband and wife should be Agape. The Gentiles—the nonbelievers, however, express Eros.

4:6 **that no one should take advantage of and defraud his brother in this matter.** When you look at your brother's wife with a lustful eye (and this applies to either spouse), you are taking advantage of your brother and defrauding him in this matter. St. Paul is reminding us with the tenth commandment, which includes the remark: *"you shall not covet your neighbor's wife"* (Ex. 20:17). We, as children of God, should be respectful of one another and not harm each other. When we lust after one another (and especially if we act on such lust), we may damage and harm others and affect their marriages. As children of God, we should protect and keep the sanctity of marriage (not only of our own but that of others as well).

brother. *"Brother"* here does not mean necessary a biological brother, but referring generally to any brothers in Christ.

✠ St. Paul gives four reasons for why we should not *"defraud"* our brother in this matter:

because the Lord is the avenger of all such. (1) of 4. All of us recall the sin of David and how God sent Nathan the Prophet to rebuke him (2 Sam. 12). When David confessed his sin, Nathan told him that the Lord forgives him, yet David was also warned that his child (with the woman with whom he sinned) would die; recall also the remark by Nathan that *"the sword shall* *never depart from your house"* (1 Sam. 12:10), and also the condemnation that as David did this with the wife of another man, so too will David's wives be taken from him (1 Sam. 12:11-12). Forgiveness did not save David from the consequences of his sin although God forgave him. Thus, *"the Lord is the avenger of all such."*

as we also forewarned you and testified. (2) of 4. It is possible that St. Paul forewarned the Thessalonians by mentioning the story of David (see previous remark above) and how God was an avenger of this sin.

4:7 **For God did not call us to uncleanness, but in holiness.** (3) of 4. We should not engage in sexual immorality and take advantage of one another because we were called to live a holy life and a life of sanctification: *"For this is the will of God, your sanctification"* (v.3 above). That is why we need to be very careful lest we defile our hearts and also defile others by our lusts and our sins.

❖ *These verses apply to the youth to abstain from any kind of immorality (not just sexual)* ~ The last collection of verses are not only for married people, but also for youth who many times do not keep the purity of their bodies. When speaking about the purity of our bodies it is not just sexual immorality to which I am referring, but

also defiling our bodies with drinking, dancing, drugs, or any other activities such as those. By engaging in those practices, you are killing your body, not walking in holiness or sanctification as God called you. I remember His Grace Bishop Moussa (General Bishop of Youth Affairs) once said, "Four 'D's' lead to a fifth 'D'"—the Four "'D's" are: Drinking, Drugs, Dating, & Dancing. Those four lead to Death (spiritual death). We must be careful because our sanctification is God's will for us, and he called us to walk in holiness.

4:8 **Therefore he who rejects this does not reject man, but God, who has also given us His Holy Spirit.** (4) of 4. Rejecting this teaching is as if you are rejecting God Himself. God gave us the Holy Spirit to sanctify our bodies. When we reject this teaching and live in impurity, it is as if we are casting the Holy Spirit away from our hearts and asking Him to leave us. The Holy Spirit cannot dwell in a heart that is defiled or impure.

4:9 **But concerning brotherly love you have no need that I should write to you.** It is very beautiful that the people in Thessalonica were already practicing and loving one another with *"Agape"* (see commentary of v.5 above). Loving one another is in itself a testimony that you are children of God, as the Lord Christ told us: *"By this all will know that you are My disciples, if you have love for one another"* (John 13:35). St. Paul is saying, "You do not need me to remind you or tell you about this, because you are already walking and living in love as you ought."

for you yourselves are taught by God to love one another. St. Paul is talking about the teaching that we receive directly from the Holy Spirit in our hearts, when we are sensitive to the voice of God. Thus, besides the teaching of the Church, Holy Scriptures, and spiritual fathers, a person should listen to the immediate and direct voice of the Holy Spirit in his or her heart. However, this needs practice, as St. Paul said, *"those who by reason of use have their senses exercised to discern both good and evil"* (Heb. 5:14). We must train our senses to listen to the Holy Spirit in our hearts and learn from Him.

But we urge you, brethren, that you increase more and more. Although the Thessalonians had no need to be told how to love one another, nonetheless, St. Paul urges them to grow "more and more." This means that there is always room for growth, especially in this commandment of love. "God is love" (1 John 4:8), and He is infinite, and thus, there is no limit to love. No one can claim that they reached perfection in love. In order to be perfect in love you need infinite time, because love is infinite. That is why not only here on earth, will we grow in love, but also in heaven, we will grow in love. In order to reach perfect love, we need infinite time, and so eternal life is infinite. ❖ When saying that the Colossians should *"increase more and more"* in their love, St. Paul does not speak simply of just emotion (*"Philia"*), but speaking about Agape (see v.5 above). When you read 1 Corinthians 13, you will find love in action, as St. John said: *"Let us not love in word or in tongue, but in deed and in truth"* (1 John 3:18).

4:10   and indeed you do so toward all the brethren who are in all Macedonia. Not only are the Thessalonians expressing Christian love to just those in the church of Thessalonica, but actually in the whole province of Macedonia. When the love of God grows in your heart, it will grow to an extent that it includes everyone, not just those in your inner circle but everyone, even your enemies.

4:11-12   St. Paul mentions five things here related to the notion of walking in diligence. The following provides the backdrop for why St. Paul focused on this subject. The people of Thessalonica thought that the Second Coming of the Lord Jesus Christ was going to happen very soon, as was a common thought among many in the Early Church. St. Paul wanted to make it known that this is not correct. Expecting the coming of the Lord caused many to become idle, which in turn caused a number of problems related to diminishing diligence in the faith.

4:11 **that you also aspire to lead a quiet life.** (1) of 5. You need to live a quiet life. Do not make a big show of your life, but just go to work, church, worship, and spend time with your family, friends, and that is it. When we are surrounded with a lot of noise in our lives, we often become distracted and find it hard to focus on the eternal life. As Christians, we need to be quiet and calm. God works in calmness and quietness (cf., Prov. 17:27; Mark 4:39). You cannot hear the voice of God if you are surrounded with the noise of the world. For example, when you look at water, if it is not still but moving and subject to much commotion, you cannot see your face in it. But when the water is calm and still, you can see your face. In the same way, when you are surrounded by distractions, you cannot examine your heart, and you cannot listen to the voice of God. Go to a very busy and noisy place, like a factory, and if someone you know calls for you, you probably will not recognize the sound over all the noise. However, in a calm and quiet atmosphere, even a whisper can be heard.

to mind your own business. (2) of 5. We should not be a "busybody in other people's matters" (1 Pet. 4:15). When we are not busy or if we have a lot of time on our hands, it is common that we turn to other people's matters by gossiping or interfering in their lives. This is a sin. What is interesting is that St. Peter (in the quote mentioned above), puts the sin of murder and that of being a busybody in the same sentence and on the same level: *"But let none of you suffer as a murderer, a thief, an evildoer, or as a busybody in other people's matters"* (1 Pet. 4:15). Once, when the Lord said, *"Follow Me,"* St. Peter turned around and *"saw the disciple whom Jesus loved [i.e., St. John the Beloved] following, who also had leaned on His breast at the supper."* St. *"Peter, seeing him, said to Jesus, 'But Lord, what about this man?' Jesus said to him, 'If I will that he remain till I come, what is that to you? You follow Me"* (John 21:19-22). This little story can be understood in the sense that the Lord considered St. Peter's question as if he was not minding his own business. That is why St. Peter learned this lesson, not to interfere or gossip about others, not to be a busybody. ⚜ Many times, we like to speak about others or discuss their affairs. It is not our responsibility or our job to do this. With such gossip, we fall into a lot of sins and judgment.

and to work with your own hands, as we commanded you. (3) of 5. Some people started to quit working in expectation of the Second Coming of

Christ and even started asking others to help them with their needs, but St. Paul did not support such a state of affairs. Actually, in St. Paul's second letter to the Thessalonians, we find the verse, *"If anyone will not work, neither shall he eat"* (2 Thess. 3:10). That is why if someone comes to the church and asks for financial help, if he can work, the church should not help him; otherwise, the church is encouraging people to be lazy. Even in monasticism, monks should work by their own hands; and this teaching, we learned from St. Anthony the Great who used to make baskets and sell them to eat from the work of his own hands. Thus, even the monks, who dedicate their entire lives to the worship of God, have to work and eat from their efforts.

4:12 **that you may walk properly toward those who are outside.** (4) of 5. Who are *"those who are outside"*? St. Paul is speaking here about the nonbelievers. Our conduct and behavior before those who are outside can serve as a testimony and attract them to Christianity and belief in the Lord Jesus Christ. This is as the Lord told us when He said, *"you are the salt of the earth"* (Matt. 5:13) and *"you are the light of the world ... Let your light so shine before men, that they may see your good works and glorify your Father in heaven."* (Matt. 5:14, 16). When we *"walk properly"* and let our light shine before others, this will be an

appropriate testimony and may attract people to believe in the Lord Jesus Christ. That is how we can evangelize, by our own conduct and behavior. ❈ This verse also can be understood to mean that we should deal wisely with nonbelievers. We need wisdom for this in order to win them to the true faith.

and that you may lack nothing. (5) of 5. When you work, you will not fall into financial embarrassment, whereby you cannot support your own needs and cover your own expenses, turning to others for help. God gave you the power, talents, and energy to care for your own needs and be responsible for yourself so that you lack nothing.

4:13-18 During the time of persecution, many believers from Thessalonica were killed. Those who were alive began to be sorrowful because of the martyrs. Some were sorrowful to a very hopeless extent. That is why St. Paul focused his letter on the resurrection and the coming of the Lord, so that they have hope: those who died for Christ are not dead. As we say in the Litany of the Departed, "There is no death for your servants, but a departure."

4:13 **But I do not want you to be ignorant, brethren, concerning those who have fallen asleep.** Notice here how St. Paul uses the word *"fallen asleep"* rather than *"died."* There is no death for God's servants, but a departure. Real death is eternal punishment (cf., Prov. 12:28), but physical death is not a final cessation of existence. Thus, the Lord said, *"But concerning the resurrection of the dead, have you not read what was spoken to you by God, saying, 'I am the God of Abraham, the God of Isaac, and the God of Jacob'? God is not the God of the dead, but of the living"* (Matt. 22:31-32). We communicate with the saints because we believe they are alive. Although Pope Kyrillos VI departed many years ago, yet several people until today still communicate with him and feel his presence in their lives, which is a sure sign that those who have departed to be with Christ are not dead but are alive.

lest you sorrow as others who have no hope. St. Paul is saying again, "We are not like the nonbelievers. They do not believe in the resurrection of Christ, and thus, they have no hope. But, we believe in the resurrection of Christ." Our hope is in the resurrection. Christ is the Head, and we are His body (cf., Col. 1:18; 2:10, 19); if the Head rose from the dead, then, so too will the rest of His body. But, if we are not from the body of Christ, then we will have no hope. In order to have hope in the resurrection, we need to be a part of the body of Christ, *"which is the Church"* (Col. 1:24; cf., Eph 1:23, 5:30). Thus, we should not be sorrowful like the nonbelievers who have every right to

be sorrowful as there is no hope without Christ.

4:14　For if we believe that Jesus died and rose again, even so God will bring with Him those who sleep in Jesus. If you believe in the resurrection of Christ, then all those who *"sleep in Jesus"* will also rise again. Thus, we should not be sorrowful like the nonbelievers.

sleep in Jesus. Those who are united with Christ in life will rise again, but those who are not will suffer the *"resurrection of condemnation"* (John 5:29), as the Lord Christ said.

4:15-17　St. Paul begins to focus more directly now on the sequence of events that will transpire around the time of the Second Coming of the Lord.

4:15　For this we say to you by the word of the Lord. St. Paul is relaying the notion that what he is saying is not his own personal teaching or understanding, but the teaching of the Holy Spirit.

that we who are alive and remain until the coming of the Lord will by no means precede those who are asleep. Let us imagine that the Lord

Jesus Christ came right now. For those of us who are still alive right now, who will meet the Lord first: us who are alive or those who have slept in the Lord? St. Paul is saying that those who remain alive will not *"precede"* those who have fallen asleep. Those who have died will rise first and will come on the clouds with the Lord, then, we will be caught up to meet God. St. Paul is saying to them, "Why are you so sorrowful about the martyrs and those who have slept in the Lord? They will actually come first before us who remain alive. They are in a better position (in a way) because they will precede us before we are caught up to meet the Lord."

4:16 For the Lord Himself will descend from heaven. This is the Second Coming. This reminds us with the words of the two angels to the disciples at the Mount of Ascension: *"Now when He had spoken these things, while they watched, He was taken up, and a cloud received Him out of their sight. And while they looked steadfastly toward heaven as He went up, behold, two men stood by them in white apparel, who also said, 'Men of Galilee, why do you stand gazing up into heaven? This same Jesus, who was taken up from you into heaven, will so come in like manner as you saw Him go into heaven'"* (Acts 1:9-11). Thus, the Lord will descend from heaven, accompanied by the following things:

with a shout. (1) of 3. This is a shout of joy and victory that the Lord conquered death and Satan to the end.

with the voice of an archangel. (2) of 3. This may refer to (most probably) Archangel Sorial who, by tradition, we consider as the angel known for using a trumpet. This may also refer to Archangel Michael. An archangel will come and announce the coming of the Lord.

and with the trumpet of God. (3) of 3. In the Old Testament, they used the trumpet to gather the people together. In a similar fashion, the trumpet will be used to gather the elect, whether they are alive or have already fallen asleep in Jesus.

And the dead in Christ will rise first. The dead will rise first, accompanying Christ on the clouds.

4:17 Then we who are alive and remain shall be caught up together with them in the clouds to meet the Lord in the air. Although not mentioned here, elsewhere St. Paul clarifies that those who are alive at the time of the Second Coming will first be "changed—in a moment" and then afterward we will be caught up together with the saints in the clouds to meet the Lord (*"Behold, I tell you a mystery: We shall not all sleep, but we shall all be changed—in a moment, in the twinkling* *of an eye, at the last trumpet. For the trumpet will sound, and the dead will be raised incorruptible, and we shall be changed."*—1 Cor. 15:51-52). We will change into a glorious body akin to that of the resurrected body of Christ (Phil 3:21). Then, only the believers will be caught up to meet the Lord and the saints.

❖ *The biblical teaching of "rapture"* ~ From this verse, people have conceptualized the notion of *"rapture"* in various ways. The biblical teaching of the *"rapture"* is that it happens at the time of the Second Coming of the Lord Christ, rather than as others teach, well before the Second Coming. Many Protestant denominations teach that rapture will happen before the great tribulation (which precedes the Second Coming). St. Paul is very clear here, and if you read from the Gospel according to St. Matthew, Chapter 24, you will find that rapture happens after the great tribulation, not before. This is when the believers will be caught up to meet the Lord during His Second Coming, after *"the dead in Christ ... rise first"* (v.16 above). From the Protestants, there are a series of books called "Left Behind" which is founded on non-biblical teachings, hypothesizing that the rapture will happen before the great tribulation, so that those who are left behind will suffer during the great tribulation. St. Paul made it clear that this is not his own personal teaching, but the *"word of the Lord"* (v.15 above), that the rapture will happen after the rising of the dead

and the Coming of the Lord, not before the great tribulation..

And thus we shall always be with the Lord. Recall what St. Paul said to the Philippians: *"For I am hard-pressed between the two, having a desire to depart and be with Christ, which is far better"* (Phil. 1:23). There is no greater joy than to remain always with the Lord, in His company and be one with Him.

4:18 Therefore comfort one another with these words. When we remember and live the events of the Second Coming of the Lord, keeping in mind always that He is coming again to take us with Him and to be with Him always, this brings peace and comfort to our hearts. The resurrection of the Lord and His Second Coming is what brings joy and comfort to the believers' hearts. That is why in every Divine Liturgy, we recite the Creed and conclude by saying, "We look for the resurrection of the dead and the life of the age to come." These two things are the source of comfort for all of us.

Chapter 4 Questions

1. How can a person be blameless at the time of the coming of the Lord?

2. What is the will of God?

3. Why should we abstain from sexual immorality?

4. Is there a limit for our growth in love? Why?

5. How do we walk in diligence?

6. What is the sequence of events at the time of the Second Coming of the Lord?

7. Why do we comfort one another regarding those who have fallen asleep?

5

Chapter Outline

- The Second Coming (1-3)
- Walk in light (4-11)
- Walk in obedience (12-22)
- Concluding remarks (23-28)

Introduction

St. Paul ended the previous chapter by speaking about the Second Coming (or "Parousia") of Christ, the rapture of the living believers, and the resurrection of the faithful departed. He was seeking to give hope to the Thessalonians who felt sorrowful over the death of their fellow Christians due to persecution or otherwise.

5:1 **But concerning the times and the seasons, brethren, you have no need that I should write to you.** St. Paul has no need to write to the Thessalonians about the time of the return of the Lord. It is not for us to know the time and season of the Second Coming. If you read Acts Chapter 1, you will see that the disciples asked the Lord Jesus Christ a very direct question: *"Lord, will You at this time restore the kingdom of Israel?"* (Acts 1:6). Christ replied by saying, *"It is not for you to know times or seasons which the Father has put in His own authority"*

(Acts 1:7). Therefore, the times and seasons is in the authority of the Father and not for us to know. Many people in our time nowadays are engrossed in calculating the time of our Lord Christ's Second Coming, but in actuality this is all against what the Bible teaches us. If God wants to reveal when He will come, He can announce it, and so we do not need all this preoccupation with the timing of this matter.

5:2 **For you yourselves know perfectly that the day of the Lord so comes as a thief in the night.** St. Paul explains that the coming of the Lord will come at a time when we do not expect. Thus, if it is for us to know, why would it be a surprise? It is not something about which we are to know beforehand. Recall too that after the Lord concluded the parable of the five wise and five foolish virgins, He said, *"Watch therefore, for you know neither the day nor the hour in which the Son of Man is coming"* (Matt. 25:13). This is why we should be ready all the time.
✠ St. Paul means something else by this verse as well. If you are ready, the day will not be like a thief surprising you in the night. However, if you are not ready, then you are not expecting the coming of the Lord, and thus, His Second coming will surprise you. We read in v.4 of this chapter, *"But you, brethren, are not in darkness, so that this Day should overtake you as a thief."* This Day will overtake you as a thief if you walk in darkness. Thus, since we do not know the Day in which He will

come again, we must walk in the light, which means we must be ready and watchful for His Second Coming.

5:3 **For when they say, "Peace and safety!" then sudden destruction comes upon them.** Here, St. Paul speaks specifically about sinners, since he says *"sudden destruction comes upon them."* In the Gospel according to St. Luke, we read what Christ said about this moment: *"And as it was in the days of Noah, so it will be also in the days of the Son of Man: They ate, they drank, they married wives, they were given in marriage, until the day that Noah entered the ark, and the flood came and destroyed them all. ... Even so will it be in the day when the Son of Man is revealed"* (Luke 17:26-27, 30). The people at the time of Noah were saying *"peace and safety"* and then suddenly, the flood came. In the same way it happened with Sodom and Gomorrah, *"they ate, they drank, they bought, they sold, they planted, they built,"* but then all of a sudden, *"it rained fire and brimstone from heaven and destroyed them all"* (Luke 17:28-29). That is why we must be ready and be watchful unless this Day overtake us as it happened in the days of Noah and also Lot. That is why St. Paul tells us that the evildoers will say, *"Peace and safety"* (i.e., "No, it is not going to happen any time soon. Let's just enjoy the pleasures of the world"); however, sudden destruction will come upon

them. This reminds us of the parable of Christ in which a *"certain rich man yielded plentifully,"* and when he had run out of room to store his crops and goods, he built more and more storage space until he said to his soul, *"Soul, you have many goods laid up for many years; take your ease; eat, drink, and be merry"* (Luke 12:19). But to that, *"God said to him, 'Fool! This night your soul will be required of you; then whose will those things be which you have provided?'"* (Luke 12:20). We need to be watchful and ready.

as labor pains upon a pregnant woman. St. Paul gives another example: that of the *"labor pains upon a pregnant woman."* A pregnant woman knows for sure that labor pains will come upon her, but she does not know when exactly. All of us know for sure that we will depart from this world sooner or later, and that this world will end and the Lord will come again to take us to the kingdom of Heaven. Although we know for sure that our lives here are not eternal and we will die one day or another, we will be surprised like the labor pains surprise a pregnant woman.

And they shall not escape. Who will escape the surprise of this Day? Only those who are ready will. That is why, after speaking about how we do not know the Day of the Second Coming and that we should be watchful, beginning with verse 4, he begins to teach us how to ready ourselves and be watchful for the coming of the Lord.

5:4 **But you, brethren, are not in darkness, so that this Day should overtake you as a thief.** If you *"walk in the light as He is in the light"* (1 John 1:7), the *"Day"* will not surprise you. In this context, walking in the light means two things, as explained in the following verse.

5:5-7 **You are all sons of light and sons of the day. We are not of the night nor of darkness. 6 Therefore let us not sleep, as others do, but let us watch and be sober. 7 For those who sleep, sleep at night, and those who get drunk are drunk at night.** There are two aspects of this day/night example provided by St. Paul. Firstly, people usually work during the day and sleep during the night. Walking in light means you are active in your spiritual life and are not lazy. Instead of sleeping, you are kindling your spirit. Secondly, those who commit sins (such as drinking, robbing, etc.), they usually try to do so during the darkness, so that no one will see them, hiding their sins. Walking in light, then, also refers to walking in righteousness, rather than in sin. Hence, the two things we can distill from this verse is that we must be active in our spiritual lives (rather than being lazy), and to live righteously.

watch. We must always watch out for Satan lest he plant any evil thoughts in our hearts. Let us be watchful in case Satan steals our purity and

righteousness. The true believer is always living the life of righteousness, guarding every part of himself from the attacks of Satan.

and be sober. *"Sober"* is the opposite of drunk. A drunk person does not know how to control himself or herself. That is why he or she makes irrational decisions. A sober person controls himself or herself. That is why the children of the light are aware of what they are doing and their decisions. To be righteous or not depends on the choices being made every day. You have a choice to lie or to say the truth, to be honest or not, to accept lustful thoughts or to reject them. If you are sober all the time, you will make good choices, unlike our mother Eve who made a bad decision and fell because of it.

For those who sleep, sleep at night. Night sleep resembles laziness in our spiritual lives. For example, if you are lazy to pray, to open the Bible and study the word of God, lazy to come to church and worship the Lord, lazy to go and help a poor person or a needy person, lazy to do some good work or rescue a person from sin, then, you are actually like those who *"sleep at night."* But, those who are active as if it is day are not lazy: they pray, read the Bible, go to church, helps others, and make profit for the glory of God with His gifts.

5:8 **But let us who are of the day be sober, putting on the breastplate of faith and love, and as a helmet the hope of salvation.** Here, St. Paul mentions, as he did to the Corinthians, the three main virtues: *"And now abide faith, hope, love, these three; but the greatest of these is love"* (1 Cor. 13:13). St. Paul is bringing to mind the notion of a guard on his watch who is armed and ready. How do we arm ourselves? What weapons do we need to guard our minds, hearts, and senses? St. Paul spoke about two weapons: the breastplate (which protects the heart) and the helmet (which protects the mind and thoughts).

✠ *Ignorance leading to sin* ~ What makes people sin? It is either ignorance or intentionally desiring to go astray. We say in the Gregorian Liturgy, "As a true Light, You have shone upon the ignorant and the lost." Spiritual darkness or blindness means you either do not know the word of God (which is light), and such ignorance will cause you to live a life of unrighteousness. As David the prophet said, "Your word is a lamp to my feet, and a light to my path" (Ps. 119:105). Ignorance occurs when a person does not feed his mind with the knowledge of the word of God; going astray is when someone follows the lust of one's heart. That is why we need to guard our thoughts (signified by the helmet) and our hearts (signified by the breastplate), which are the two most vital parts of our bodies that affect our lives if injured.

faith and love. Having told the Ephesians to put on the *"breastplate of righteousness"* (Eph. 6:14), the Thessalonians are told to put on the *"breastplate of faith and love."* There is no contradiction in these two phrases, but they work in harmony. Righteousness is imputed to man for justification (cf., Rom. 4:11, 5:16)—coming by *"faith [i.e., motive from within] and working through love [i.e., outward acts]"* (Gal. 5:6). When we have true faith from within and our works on the outside are for the glory of God, then we will be righteous. Righteousness means doing what is right, but it must be for the right purpose and out of the right motive. Many do what is right as hypocrites to receive glory from men. But, doing what is right is to act righteously founded on the right motive. Out of the proper motive of love should ensue: *"let us not love in word or in tongue, but in deed and in truth"* (1 Jn. 3:18).

the hope of salvation. To protect your mind, you need to ponder all the time on the hope of salvation, which will keep you motivated to fight the spiritual warfare. That is why St. Paul says we need to put on the helmet of the hope of salvation. What makes a student motivated to succeed is the hope for success. What makes the worker work so hard is the hope of making a lot of profit. For a farmer, it is the hope of the harvest. In the same way, when the hope of salvation fills our minds and our thoughts, this will help us remain motivated to work hard to be children of the day and not children of the night.

5:9 For God did not appoint us to wrath, but to obtain salvation. This is a very important verse. After mentioning the hope of salvation, he says, *"God did not appoint us to wrath, but to obtain salvation."* God did not prepare the lake of fire for us, but rather for Satan and his evil angels *("For ... God did not spare the angels who sinned, but cast them down to hell and delivered them into chains of darkness, to be reserved for judgment."*—2 Peter 2:4). Christ tells us that the kingdom was prepared from the foundation of the world for us, while everlasting fire was prepared for the devil and his angels: *"Then the King will say to those on His right hand, 'Come, you blessed of My Father, inherit the kingdom prepared for you from the foundation of the world'"* (Matt. 25:34); *"Then He will also say to those on the left hand, 'Depart from Me, you cursed, into the everlasting fire prepared for the devil and his angels'"* (Matt. 25:41). Although God did not prepare punishment for people, but rather for the devil and his angels, unfortunately, those who follow in the way of the devil will have a share in his inheritance in everlasting fire. Thus, we are told, *"work out your own salvation with fear and trembling"* (Phil. 2:12). God created you to inherit the kingdom of Heaven, telling us, *"Do not fear, little flock, for it is your Father's good*

pleasure to give you the kingdom" (Luke 12:32).

through our Lord Jesus Christ. *"Let it be known to you all ... that by the name of Jesus Christ of Nazareth, whom you crucified, whom God raised from the dead ... There [is no] salvation in any other, for there is no other name under heaven given among men by which we must be saved"* (Acts 4:10, 12). When you believe in Christ and submit your life to Him, following His steps, then you will obtain eternal salvation.

who died for us. Christ died for us to pay the punishment of sin. He died on our behalf in order to save us and redeem us. That is why we are appointed for salvation and not for wrath. He took our sins upon Himself and became a curse for us: *"Christ has redeemed us from the curse of the law, having become a curse for us"* (Gal. 3:13). Wrath already fell upon Christ on the cross in order to deliver us from wrath.

that whether we wake or sleep, we should live together with Him. This refers to the Second Coming of the Lord, whether those who are alive at that time or those who had already died (see commentary on 1 Thess. 4:17). St. Paul wants to comfort the Thessalonians for those who had died due to persecution, indicating that those who die or remain alive until the Second Coming of the Lord, all of us will be caught up to meet the Lord on the cloud to live with Him.

5:11 **Therefore comfort each other and edify one another, just as you also are doing.** When we reflect upon and always meditate on the Second Coming of our Lord, it brings comfort and peace to our hearts. It also helps us to grow and be edified. That is why we have a responsibility to one another (*"just as you also are doing"*) to remind each other of the Second Coming of the Lord—reminding one another that we should walk in light because we are sons of light and sons of day, not sons of darkness. When we remind one another, we will be comforted and motivated to grow more and more in our spiritual lives.

5:12-13 **And we urge you, brethren, to recognize those who labor among you, and are over you in the Lord and admonish you, and to esteem them very highly in love for their work's sake.** St. Paul is speaking about spiritual fathers when he refers to *"those who labor among you, and are over you in the Lord and admonish you."* Some scholars of the Bible consider this reference to signify the three ranks of the priesthood: (1) *"Those who labor among you"* as referring to deacons, because the deacons' role is to serve; and the word deacon means ministry or service. (2) Those who *"are over you"* referring to the bishops, whose original Greek title is Episcopos (overseer). (3) Those who *"admonish you"* is regarded as

referring to the priests, whose role it is to admonish the people and instruct people in the Lord.

✤ *The responsibilities of the clergy toward their flock:*

labor. (1) of 3. It is the responsibility of the clergy to *"labor,"* which means to work hard in order to satisfy the needs of the flock. Here, I recall the words of His Holiness Pope Shenouda III whenever he ordained priests or bishops. He would usually tell them, if you labor and work hard, people will have rest, but if you rest and become lazy, people will suffer. That is the first responsibility of the clergy.

are over you. (2) of 3. This means that God gave the priesthood authority, but it is not to rule over the people, but to protect the flock. Authority in Christianity, when given by God to someone, is usually to serve and protect and guard, not to rule over others. The Lord distinguished authority in the concept of nonbelievers from those who are believers in Him, when He said, *"You know that those who are considered rulers over the Gentiles lord it over them, and their great ones exercise authority over them. Yet it shall not be so among you; but whoever desires to become great among you shall be your servant. And whoever of you desires to be first shall be slave of all. For even the Son of Man did not come to be served, but to serve, and to give His life a ransom for many"*

(Mark 10:42-45). In marriage too, for example, authority to the husband is not to control and rule over his wife but to protect and guard his wife

admonish you. (3) of 3. This includes the notion of instructing as well as disciplining. King David says, in Psalm 23, *"Your rod and Your staff, they comfort me"* (Ps. 23:4). The rod is for disciplining, and the staff for shepherding. Admonishing here means to instruct and also to discipline. There is no contradiction in protecting the flock and disciplining them. *"If you endure chastening, God deals with you as with sons; for what son is there whom a father does not chasten? But if you are without chastening, of which all have become partakers, then you are illegitimate and not sons. Furthermore, we have had human fathers who corrected us, and we paid them respect. Shall we not much more readily be in subjection to the Father of spirits and live? For they indeed for a few days chastened us as seemed best to them, but He for our profit, that we may be partakers of His holiness. Now no chastening seems to be joyful for the present, but painful; nevertheless, afterward it yields the peaceable fruit of righteousness to those who have been trained by it"* (Heb. 12:7-11). If we reject discipline then we are not children. If a father loves his son, he disciplines him. Part of protecting the flock is disciplining the sheep to bring them back.

✤ *The responsibilities of the flock toward their clergy:*

recognize. (1) of 3. This means that you should recognize their office and calling, and their appointment by God to have authority, and treating them accordingly with their due reverence. *"He who hears you hears Me, he who rejects you rejects Me, and he who rejects Me rejects Him who sent Me"* (Luke 10:16); *"Most assuredly, I say to you, he who receives whomever I send receives Me; and he who receives Me receives Him who sent Me"* (John 13:20). Our reverence for the clergy should extend also to supplying liberally for their needs, for they have left everything to serve the Lord.

to esteem them very highly ... for their work's sake. (2) of 3. We esteem our spiritual fathers for whom they represent, i.e., representing God. St. Paul says that we are *"ambassadors for Christ"* (2 Cor. 5:20) and *"stewards of the mysteries of God"* (1 Cor. 4:1). It is not because of who they are but of whom they represent and their calling. Their work for our sake is the furtherance of our salvation and the kingdom of Christ.

in love. (3) of 3. We should esteem our spiritual fathers out of love, not out of a spirit of hypocrisy or simply flattering lips (cf., Ps. 12:2). Our love towards our spiritual fathers is a love of Christ who appointed them to this position.

Be at peace among yourselves. Do not only keep peace between you and the clergy, but also among the flock. And therefore, we hear the deacon in every Divine Liturgy tell the people to "Greet one another with a holy kiss." All of us are members of the same body of Christ and must live in peace with one another. If we live in conflict and division, then as the Lord said, *"Every city or house divided against itself will not stand"* (Matt. 12:25). In the Church of God, everyone lives in peace together.

5:14 Now we exhort you, brethren.

St. Paul speaks of three different types of disobedient people and tells us how to deal with them— those who are unruly, fainthearted, and weak.

warn those who are unruly. St. Paul, here, refers to those who do not follow the rules. God is a God of order, not of chaos: *"For God is not the author of confusion but of peace, as in all the churches of the saints"* (1 Cor. 14:33). Therefore, we are told by St. Paul, *"Let all things be done decently and in order"* (1 Cor. 14:140). Many people like to challenge the rules, especially those of the church. When you live in a country or work for a company, you respect the rules of that country or workplace. But, when it comes to the church, people often like to challenge the church rules, following their own rules or imposing their own rules on others. St. Paul says that we should *"warn"* the unruly, because they are walking in disobedience. ✠ *"Unruly"* has another meaning. Some people thought that the coming of the Lord would be very soon. Thus, many quit working and started to focus on the coming of the Lord. They did not have money and asked others to provide for their needs. St. Paul considered this predicament to be unruly, whereby they were transgressing the rule that, *"If anyone will not work, neither shall he eat"* (2 Thess. 3:10). That is why, when some people come to the church and ask for help, if the church finds them work and they refuse to work and still insist to receive help from the church, then the church should not help those people, because if the church is helping those who do not want to work, then the church is encouraging wrong behavior. The church's responsibility is to *"warn"* the unruly.

comfort the fainthearted. The *"fainthearted"* are those who have not set their mind on the hope of salvation (cf., v.8 above). Thus, during persecution, they became very fearful and scared, and may deny the Lord Jesus Christ. This is why St. Paul says to *"comfort"* them, letting them know that Christ promised us, *"I will never leave you nor forsake you"* (Heb. 13:5).

uphold the weak. The *"weak"* are those who want to do, but do not have the strength to do it. They have the will, but they do not act upon that will. Usually, they need support. For example, you may find someone who says "I want to pray, read the Bible, and go to church," but the person (although their will and intention is good), does not actually put his or her intentions into actual actions. Thus, if we meet someone with a good will but lacks strength, we have a responsibility to uphold and support him or her so that he or she can act on his or her will.

be patient with all. Everyone needs patience. Everyone deserves another chance. We should be longsuffering with everyone. If God were not patient with us, we would not still exist now. But, it is because of His patience that after we rebelled against Him, He saved us; and until now, although we rebel several times against Him, when we return to Him, He accepts all of us. That is why, if God is so patient with us, we must be patient with each other. Imagine if a husband is truly patient with his wife and vice versa, parents with their children and vice versa, bosses with their employees and the opposite, we would be living such a heavenly life. When we are impatient and lose our temper quickly, that is why we have so much conflict with one another. But, if we learn to be patient and to wait for one another, we will live in peace.

5:15 See that no one renders evil for evil to anyone. After mentioning patience just before this verse, St. Paul gives us some practical application for the principle of patience. If someone insults you, do not render evil for evil. That is how to be patient with one another. I am sure you have heard the story of "Moalem" Ibrahim El Gohery. A nonbeliever used to always curse and act wickedly with Moalem Ibrahim's brother, who eventually told Moalem Ibrahim what was going on. Moalem Ibrahim said, "Don't worry, I will stop him completely from insulting you." The next day, Moalem Ibrahim sent many gifts to the person that was insulting his brother, indicating that the gifts were actually from Moalem Ibrahim's brother. The nonbeliever who received those gifts felt very embarrassed. The following day, instead of insulting Moalem Ibrahim's brother, he thanked and praised him for such kindness. This is as St. Paul teaches us, *"Do not be overcome by evil, but overcome evil with good"* (Rom. 12:21).

but always pursue what is good both for yourselves and for all. We must always pursue what is good for the believers, and those who are not Christian. As children of God, do good with everyone, *"for He makes His sun rise on the evil and on the good, and sends rain on the just and on the unjust"* (Matt. 5:45). If we are sons of the Father, we must do good to everyone. If we, however, render evil for evil, then, we are similar to them. What we need is to repay evil with good (Rom. 12:21), which is a sign of patience.

5:16 Rejoice always, pray without ceasing, in everything give thanks.
These three verses are three commandments which we should follow all the time. We need to be happy always, pray at all times, and give thanks in everything (which is an attitude, more than it is words, and thus, we should be grateful all the time). There is a link between these three commandments. In the Gospel according to St. John, the Lord says, *"Ask, and you will receive, that your joy may be full"* (John 16:24). The Lord is saying, when you pray, answers to your prayer will lead to joy; and when a person is joyful, he or she will give thanks; giving thanks to God is done in prayer. Thus, prayer leads to joy, which leads to thanksgiving, which leads to prayer, in a constant cycle. These three commandments should be present in us always.

for this is the will of God in Christ Jesus for you.
God wants us to be joyful and also to be peaceful (*"My peace I give to you."*—John 14:27). He wants us to be happy all of the time. The emotions of grief and sorrow are not from God, but God's children should be joyful even during hardships and suffering. As you probably know, St. Paul's letter to the Philippians was written while he was suffering in prison, but this letter is called the letter of joy in which each chapter the word joy (in that or some derivative form) was repeated more than once, and in which he wrote, *"Rejoice in the Lord always. Again I will say, rejoice!"* (Phil. 4:4). Our joy should not depend on outside circumstances, but rather it should emanate from within, because it is the fruit of the Spirit (Gal. 5:22). Outward circumstances are changeable, and if our joy is dependent on that, then so too, will be our joy; but if your joy comes from the unchangeable God, then your joy will remain always.

5:19 Do not quench the Spirit.
In Galatians 5:22, St. Paul said, *"The fruit of the Spirit is love, joy, peace, longsuffering, kindness, goodness, faithfulness."* If we quench the spirit, then we will not bear the fruit of joy. Thus, if we want to be joyful all of the time, we must not quench the Holy Spirit. We must not resist the Spirit, or counteract His influence in us. When the Spirit of God rebukes, convicts, and instructs us to do something, we must respond accordingly. Disobeying the word of God (which is inspired by the Holy Spirit), quenches the Spirit. This is so also when we refuse to follow the exhortations of the Spirit, or suppress our own consciences through which the Holy Spirit rebukes us.

5:20-21 **Do not despise prophecies. Test all things; hold fast what is good.** St. Paul, here, means inspired teaching. A prophet is one who has a message of God to us. That is what prophecy means. Not despising prophecies is not despising the inspired teachings of the Church. However, we should distinguish between true prophecies and false prophecies, just as it is said that there are true prophets and false prophets. Thus, we are told to *"test all things,"* which means we must examine and differentiate between false teachings or inspired teachings.

5:22 **Abstain from every form of evil.** False teachers and false prophets are a form of evil. Thus, we must abstain from every form of evil. Do not say, "It does not matter, they are speaking the word of God and I know the difference between different teachings and different denominations. I will listen to them since I am aware of the differences and will distinguish what is correct or not." St. Paul says, "No, abstain from every form of evil."

✠ *Christians should be particularly careful to abstain from evil* ~ A Christian should abstain not only from evil, but *"every form of evil,"* including things that have even the slightest semblance of evil (or resemblance of evil). We must be very careful, because many evils will come to us in sheep's clothing, although therein lies a

ravenous wolf (see Matt. 7:15). That is why we must be careful, by testing them against the truth of the word of God and the teachings of the Church, to distinguish between the wolf that is coming in sheep's clothing, and the true Shepherd (John 10:11, 14). Maybe something is not evil through and through, but may lead to evil; refraining from these things is included in St. Paul's request that we *"abstain from every form of evil."*

5:23 **Now may the God of peace Himself sanctify you completely.** When St. Paul calls upon the *"God of peace,"* we are reminded that the Thessalonians suffered persecution and needed the peace of God. God, the King of Peace (cf., Heb. 7:2), is able to give Him peace which surpasses all understanding. He will do this in you and sanctify you completely. It is as if St. Paul is saying that sanctification in every respect is a prerequisite for the peace of God. When God sanctifies us completely in our hearts and in our souls, then we will receive the peace of God. *"'There is no peace,' says the LORD, 'for the wicked'"* (Is. 48:22). If you want to have the peace of God, you need to be sanctified.

and may your whole spirit, soul, and body ... at the coming of our Lord Jesus Christ. Here, notice that in the resurrection of the Last Day, we rise as complete human beings: spirit, soul, and body. Yes, we will be in a glorified nature, but our entire being will be raised.

be preserved blameless. This means free from carnal (body), sensual (soul), and spiritual (spirit) sins. Everyone commits sin, so how will be blameless? It is by washing our sins in the blood of the Lord Jesus Christ, through the Sacrament of Confession and also of Communion. The purpose of these two sacraments is to wash ourselves from every carnal, sensual, and spiritual sin. In this way, when the Lord comes He will find us blameless (*"These are the ones who come out of the great tribulation, and washed their robes and made them white in the blood of the Lamb."*—Rev. 7:14).

5:24 He who calls you is faithful, who also will do it. Do not lose hope. God will sanctify you and keep you blameless. Just surrender yourself to Him. He called you and is faithful, so do not lose hope. He called us and will do it for us, but just do not resist His work or quench His Spirit.

5:25-28 In these four verses you will find a liturgical tone to them, reminiscent of what you hear in the Divine Liturgy, as seen in each verse below.

5:25 Brethren, pray for us. This reminds us of the intercessory prayers in the Liturgy (such as the Litanies including the one in which we pray for our patriarch, bishops, priests, and deacons). Where did we receive the notion of such intercessory prayers? It is from the teachings of St. Paul.

5:26 Greet all the brethren with a holy kiss. This is probably obvious in that we almost use the same words, asking the people to *"Greet one another with a holy kiss."* This is an action signifying that we are in peace with one another. We cannot be in peace with God unless we are in peace with one another.

5:27 I charge you by the Lord that this epistle be read to all the holy brethren. This is the public reading of Scripture, which we do in every Divine Liturgy. We specifically have a "Pauline" reading (i.e., a selection of one of St. Paul's letters) in every single Liturgy. Thus, through the inspiration of the Holy Spirit, we are charged to read his epistle publicly.

5:28 The grace of our Lord Jesus Christ be with you. Amen. This is the benediction. Every Divine

Liturgy is concluded by these words of benediction: "The love of God the Father; the grace of the only-begotten Son, our Lord, God, and Savior Jesus Christ; and the communion and gift of the Holy Spirit, be with you all. Go in peace. The peace of the Lord be with you all." [or simply, "The grace of our Lord, God, and Savior Jesus Christ be with you all. Go in peace. The Lord be with you all."]

Chapter 5 Questions

1. Why do the Thessalonians have no need for St. Paul to write to them concerning the times and the seasons?

2. What does it mean to be sons of day and sons of light?

3. How do we prepare ourselves for the coming of the Lord?

4. What are the responsibilities of the clergy and of the flock toward each other?

5. What is the relation between prayer, joy, and thanksgiving?

6. Explain the liturgical tone in this chapter.

St. Paul's Second Epistle to the
Thessalonians

AUTHOR: St. Paul. As is clear from the first verse, it is St. Paul who wrote this letter. He mentioned Timothy and Silvanus (who is also known as Silas), because they helped establish the church in Thessalonica.

PLACE & TIME: This letter was likey written in the city of Corinth around 53 A.D. (approximately one year after St. Paul wrote the first epistle).

THEME

The theme of this letter is how to be steadfast while waiting for the Lord, particularly when it comes to maintaining apostolic traditions rather than the traditions of men.

PURPOSE

The purpose of this letter is to relay three messages:

St. Paul wanted to praise the Thessalonians for their growth and faith in love, and for their steadfastness in enduring persecution.

Moreover, many people misunderstood the persecution they were suffering as being an immediate precursor to Christ's Second Coming (considering it to be the tribulation that comes at the end of days), to the extent that some people quit their work and lived off the charity of the people in the church. St. Paul wanted to correct their misunderstanding about the Second Coming of the Lord and confirm them in the apostolic faith, refuting the traditions of men that taught the misconception of Christ's Second Coming in the first place.

Finally, St. Paul wanted to instruct them regarding the notion of work and to motivate them not to be lazy (since many people quit working expecting Christ's Second Coming to be very soon).

HISTORICAL BACKGROUND

The church in Thessalonica was founded around 50 A.D. during St. Paul's second missionary trip. It was composed mainly of Gentiles (non-Jewish people) who experienced persecution by their fellow citizens. Because of such persecution, they thought this was the time of the Great Tribulation that would come before the Second Coming of the Lord. Many people quit working to wait for the coming of the lord.

1

Chapter Outline

- Salutation (1-2)
- Thanksgiving (3-4)
- The righteous judgment of God (5-10)
- His prayer for them (11-12)

1:1 Paul, Silvanus, and Timothy. St. Paul mentions Timothy and Silvanus (also known as Silas) because they helped in establishing the church of the Thessalonians.

To the church of the Thessalonians. The letter is here marked as being addressed to the Thessalonians.

in God our Father and the Lord Jesus Christ. Every church that is founded must be founded on God the Father and His Son the Lord Jesus Christ, as St. Paul wrote to the Corinthians: *"For we are God's fellow workers; you are God's field, you are God's building. According to the grace of God which was given to me, as a wise master builder I have laid the foundation, and another builds on it. But let each one take heed how he builds on it. For no other foundation can anyone lay than that which is laid, which is Jesus Christ"* (1 Cor. 3:9-11).

1:2 Grace to you and peace from God our Father and the Lord Jesus Christ. Grace and peace are the most needed gifts for any believer. Grace is the help from God, without which we can achieve nothing. Peace allows us to have joy and calmness especially in the midst of tribulation. If you understand that the church in Thessalonica was facing tribulation, it makes sense why they are in special need of grace and peace. Grace is needed for us to experience God's peace (when we receive the grace of God, it will be easy for us to experience His peace).

1:3 We are bound to thank God always for you, brethren, as it is fitting. St. Paul gives thanks to God about the Thessalonians for their spiritual progress. The priest or the bishop, when hearing good news about the people, should "always" give glory to God. "As it is fitting" reminds us that thanksgiving is more than words but is an attitude of appreciation and gratefulness to God—a life of thanksgiving to God. St. Paul gives thanks to God for three reasons:

because your faith grows exceedingly. (1) of 3 – Their faith grows exceedingly. We expect that with persecution the faith of people will begin to diminish and grow weaker, but in actuality the opposite happened with the Thessalonians. Their faith grew exceedingly. St. Paul understood that this was the grace of God that supported the Thessalonians during their tribulations, and thus, thanks God.

and the love of every one of you all abounds toward each other. (2) of 3 – Their love abounding toward each other as instructed in the first letter to them. In the first letter to the Thessalonians, St. Paul wrote to them saying, *"May the Lord make you increase and abound in love to one another and to all"* (1 Thess. 3:12). Apparently, the people responded to this message well so that *"the love of every one of [them] all"* (each person in the church of Thessalonica, as St. Paul very specifically mentioned) demonstrated the love St. Paul wanted to see from them. There was no conflict and division in the church, but everyone demonstrated Christian love. This is a sign of our discipleship in the Lord, as He said, *"By this all will know that you are My disciples, if you have love for one another"* (John 13:35). This love to one another shows that we are the children of God.

they cannot do all those things except by the grace of God, St. Paul began (in v.3) by giving credit to God saying, *"We are bound to thank God always for you."* St. Paul felt an obligation to give proper recognition to God rather than to himself (which he could have done saying that it was his preaching and ministry to them that resulted in their spiritual progress). .

so that we ourselves boast of you among the churches of God. When St. Paul visited other churches, St. Paul shared with them the news about the faith, love, and patient endurance of tribulation that the Thessalonians exhibited. Why? First, to set an example for other churches that this is what God wants from us. Also, St. Paul wanted to encourage others to have the same love, faith, and endurance of the Thessalonians. When there is good news, it is good to share it in order to put people in good spirits and also to help motivate others to grow in their own spiritual life.

1:4 **for your patience and faith in all your persecutions and tribulations that you endure.** (3) of 3 – Their faith and endurance of all the persecution and tribulations they faced. The Thessalonians persevered and were patiently enduring all that befell them. They neither complained nor denied their faith. Understanding that

1:5 **which is manifest evidence of the righteous judgment of God, that you may be counted worthy of the kingdom of God, for which you also suffer.** St. Paul is telling them, "Your endurance of suffering is manifest evidence that the judgment of God is righteous (that His judgment is fair)." The fact that the Thessalonians were enduring suffering means that they were waiting for something better, knowing that God will reward them in the future—the inheritance of the Kingdom of God. Unless the Thessalonians believed in the righteous judgment and compensation of God, they would not endure suffering. ❖ This reminds me of the parable of Lazarus and the Rich Man (Luke 16:19-31). If that story ended simply upon their death, it would just be a very sad story with no purpose, justice, or righteousness. However, if we look at their lives after their death, we see the Rich Man with a very hard heart and no compassion on Lazarus' suffering, while Lazarus, who endured so much suffering during his life on earth, is comforted. This story then makes sense and provides *"manifest evidence of the righteous judgment of God."*

1:6   since it is a righteous thing with God to repay with tribulation those who trouble you. As we say in the Divine Liturgy, "He appointed a day for recompense on which He will appear to judge the world in righteousness and give each one according to his deeds ("whether good or evil"—addition found in Liturgy of St. Cyril). Those who persecute the Thessalonians will be repaid for their actions.

❖   *How we should react when our Church suffers* ~ Many times when we hear of people persecuting or troubling the Church and its people, and we see

that those responsible do not receive just punishment for their actions, we feel angry. But if you think about the righteous judgment of God and trust the Lord will repay everyone according to his deeds, instead of anger, we should feel sadness for them because they are not aware of what is awaiting them in the eternal life hereafter. We are His children, and anyone who troubles us, it is as if they are troubling the Lord Jesus Christ Himself.

1:7   and to give you who are troubled rest with us. Those who endure, however, will be repaid with rest. Recall how it says in the Book of Revelation, that *"God will wipe away every tear from their eyes; there shall be no more death, nor sorrow, nor crying. There shall be no more pain, for the former things have passed away"* (Rev. 21:4). God will compensate us for the suffering and troubles, with rest if we endure. ❖ For due compensation, we must wait for the day when God comes from heaven to judge the world in righteousness. Maybe now there appears to be a lack of fairness, but when the Last Day comes, all will be recompensed fairly.

when the Lord Jesus is revealed from heaven with His mighty angels. See how St. Paul describes the Second Coming of the Lord. Christ will appear coming from heaven with His mighty angels in flaming fire. Those angels will be executing the righteous judgment of God (see also Matt. 13:49-50—*"So it will be at the end of the age. The angels will come forth, separate the wicked from among the just, and cast them into the furnace of fire. There will be wailing and gnashing of teeth."*).

1:8 in flaming fire taking vengeance. The Bible describes God as a *"consuming fire"* (Ex. 24:17; Deut. 4:24, 9:3; Heb. 12:29). This fire can be interpreted either as the fire of His glory (as He appeared to Moses in the manner of a burning bush [Ex. 3], or this can be likened to the fire of God's wrath). Personally, I prefer to interpret this fire as one of wrath since the verse continues, *"taking vengeance on those who do not know God."* ❖ Do you recall the story of Nadab and Abihu (Lev. 10), the sons of Aaron, who *"offered profane fire before the Lord"* (Lev. 10:1)? In response, a *"fire went out from the Lord and devoured them, and they died before the Lord"* (Lev. 10:2). That is the fire of vengeance.

❖ God's fire of vengeance in the Last Day will be upon two groups:

on those who do not know God. (1) of 2. This refers to the nonbelievers. You may ask, why will God destroy these people? They have an excuse, right? The answer is no, as St. Paul said, because the knowledge of God is in their hearts: *"For the wrath of God is revealed from heaven against all ungodliness and unrighteousness of men, who suppress the truth in unrighteousness, because what may be known of God is manifest in them, for God has shown it to them. For since the creation of the world His invisible attributes are clearly seen, being understood by the things that are made, even His eternal power and Godhead, so that they are without excuse, because, although they knew God, they did not glorify Him as God, nor were thankful, but became futile in their thoughts, and their foolish hearts were darkened"* (Rom. 1:18-21). Nature declares the glory of God. If we simply look at the cosmos and nature around us, we will know there is a creator. Also, God placed in us a conscience to lead us to the knowledge of Him and to tell us what is right and wrong (which people lived by before even receiving the law of Moses). Because such people did not learn about God from what was readily visible, God's vengeance will be upon them.

and on those who do not obey the gospel of our Lord Jesus Christ. (2) of 2. This refers to believers who accepted Christ, but nonetheless, chose not to obey the gospel. Faith requires obedience and is fulfilled through works. Works is the obedience of God's gospel, which is needed to fulfill His commandments.

1:9 **These shall be punished with everlasting destruction.** Both groups mentioned in the previous verse will be *"punished with everlasting destruction."* Some heresies say that such people will be punished for a temporary time after which God will forgive them and then they will be transferred to the Kingdom of God. But here, the Bible teaches us otherwise. The Greek word used here for *"everlasting"* also means "infinite" (it has no end). Thus, this heresy of temporary punishment is not biblical.

from the presence of the Lord and from the glory of His power. If you recall in Matthew Chapter 25, the Lord said to the wicked people, *"Depart from Me, you cursed, into the everlasting fire prepared for the devil and his angels"* (Matt. 25:41). Those who are wicked will not enjoy the presence of the Lord and His coming again with power.

✤ *We live because of the mercies of God* ~ To be written. One time, a youth came to me and said, "I do not want to go to heaven because I feel very bored when I pray in the church, read the bible, pray from the Agpeya, or pray the midnight praises. But when I say, 'I want to go to heaven,' I say so because the other option is so bad. Maybe if there is a third option, it would be good for me. I definitely do not want to be punished in eternal fire, but I also do not think I will enjoy heaven." So I told him, "If we assume, just for the sake of discussion, that there is a third place which is not heaven or hell, but in this place God does not exist [by which I mean the mercies of God does not exist in this place], then think about whether you want to be in such a place." See, here on earth, we enjoy the mercies of God, which is upon the righteous and the sinners. Without His grace, we cannot survive a fraction of a second. If there is a third place that is void of the mercies of God, can you imagine if His mercies were withheld for just a fraction of a second? The whole world would end." So I told him, "In this place, the people there will suffer greatly because of the lack of the mercies of God, which will be a place like hell, the everlasting fire." The main suffering that people will suffer in hell is not the torture (which will definitely be there), but rather the absence of the mercies of God. We cannot imagine surviving a fraction of a second without the mercies of God. The breath that you take is because of the mercy of God. The sun, the moon, and how the universe is being kept in perfect balance, is all because of the mercies of God. Think of even the slightest imbalances in nature and the greatest of disasters. What keeps everything in balance? It is the mercies of God. Any place that lacks that is hell. This is what we can understand when St. Paul says that those who will be designated to everlasting punishment will depart "from the presence of the Lord." They will not enjoy His power and glory, and will not be glorified.

1:10 **when He comes, in that Day.** The Second Coming of the Lord will be a day of everlasting destruction for evildoers (those who do not know God, and those who knew Him but disobeyed His gospel). But the same day will also be a day of glory and transfiguration for those who believed in God and obeyed His gospel.

to be glorified in His saints and to be admired among all those who believe. God will be glorified in us *"in that Day"* through His works and also the salvation that He fulfilled in us. He will glorify us with Him. Recall on the mountain during Christ's Transfiguration, both Moses and Elijah appeared in similar glory. So also, we will be glorified with Christ and appear to Him. People will admire God and bless His name because of His wonderful works in us, as we chant in Psalm 150, *"Praise God in all His saints"* (cf., Ps. 148:14). God will thus be glorified. *"He took what is ours to give us what is His" [as it says in the well known phrase].*

because our testimony among you was believed. This is so because the Thessalonians believed and followed what was preached to them. Thus, while they suffer persecution now, they will be transfigured in the Last Day and be glorified with Him.

1:11 **Therefore we also pray always for you.** After focusing on the Second Coming with God's fire of vengeance as well as the recompense given to the righteous who have troubled rest, St. Paul prays for all of us that we will be found worthy of enjoying heaven and being in the presence of God's glory. ❖ This is the function of the clergy, to always pray for their people. ❖ St. Paul prays for three things:

that our God would count you worthy of this calling. (1) of 3. St. Paul prays that the Thessalonians will be counted worthy of God's calling, to be worthy of being called His children.

and fulfill all the good pleasure of His goodness. (2) of 3. The good pleasure of the goodness of God is our salvation. St. Paul is thus praying that God will fulfill our salvation. Without Him, we cannot fulfill our salvation, and thus, we need to submit ourselves to Him.

and the work of faith with power. (3) of 3. See here that St. Paul used the phrase *"work of faith,"* because without works, faith is dead. We cannot do the works of faith without God, for as the Lord tells us, *"without Me you can do nothing"* (John 15:5).

1:12 **that the name of our Lord Jesus Christ may be glorified in you, and you in Him, according to the grace of our God and the Lord Jesus Christ.** The ultimate goal of the aforementioned prayer is that *"the name of our Lord Jesus Christ may be glorified"* in us, and we may be glorified in Him. The name of Christ will be glorified through fulfilling the work of Christ. We become glorified in Him when we receive the grace of God the Father and the Lord Jesus Christ. As *"heirs of God and joint heirs with Christ, if indeed we suffer with Him, ... [then we will] be glorified together"* (Rom. 8:17); *"As you are partakers of the sufferings, so also you will partake of the consolation"* (2 Cor. 1:7).

Chapter 1 Questions

1. For what did St. Paul give thanks regarding the Thessalonians?

2. How is their endurance of persecution evidence of the righteous judgment of God?

3. Describe the Second Coming of Christ?

4. Upon whom will the vengeance of God come?

5. What is the main punishment of sinners?

6. For what did St. Paul pray?

7. How can we be counted worthy for the kingdom of God and His calling?

2

Chapter Outline

Introduction

The church in Thessalonica faced persecution, and some thought this was the *"great tribulation"* (Matt. 24:21) that was to come before the Second Coming of the Lord Christ. That is why some of them had the impression that the Day of the Lord had come. Thus, in this chapter, St. Paul tried to explain to them that the day of the Lord has not yet come. He indicates that there are two signs that must happen first before the Second Coming of Christ: apostasy and the revelation of the man of sin (the Antichrist). St. Paul warned the people about the deception of the Antichrist and warned them not to be deceived, because those who do not love the truth will be easily deceived. In the conclusion of this chapter, St. Paul encouraged the Thessalonians to abide in the truth and to hold on to Holy Tradition.

2:1   Now, brethren, concerning the coming of our Lord Jesus Christ

and our gathering together to Him. The first observation one may make here is that St. Paul links together the Second Coming with our gathering together to Christ. The *"gathering together"* spoken of here is known as "rapture." Here, it is clear that the rapture is going to happen at the same time of the Second Coming. This is very important, because many Protestant denominations teach that rapture will occur before the great tribulation and before the Second Coming of Christ. The belief is that God will take up His elect so that they will not suffer through the great tribulation (Matt. 24:21). Those who are left behind will face the great tribulation, after which the Second Coming of the Lord is said will occur. However, if you study the Bible carefully, there are many verses that confirm that the rapture of Christians and the Second Coming will happen at the same time. This is one of the verses that refutes the Protestant teachings to the contrary. There is a series of books called "Left Behind," which is based on the erroneous understanding of rapture as happening before the great tribulation. The proper understanding of the timing of the rapture is clarified in this verse, as well as in 1 Thessalonians 4:17.

we ask you. St. Paul pleads with the Christians in Thessalonica.

2:2   not to be soon shaken in mind or troubled, ... as though the day of Christ had come. St. Paul understands that there are many false teachers who will try to preach that the coming of the Lord is at hand, and will even set certain dates, although the Lord Jesus Christ made it very clear when He said, *"It is not for you to know times or seasons which the Father has put in His own authority"* (Acts 1:7). Any effort to try to predict the time of the Second Coming is in opposition to the authority present only in the Father. Unfortunately, many preachers nowadays try to teach that we are in the Last Days and the Second Coming of the Lord is at hand.

either by spirit or by word or by letter, as if from us. False teaching can come by way of false revelation. Maybe someone will say they saw a vision and they were told the date of the Second Coming of the Lord. St. Paul clearly indicates that we should not be moved by such false teaching. Such falsity can be promulgated by means of preaching (*"word"*) as well as writings (*"letter"*). St. Paul warns us against all the forms of false teaching, regardless from where they are derived. However, we should "not be soon shaken," but rather, as St. Paul tells us in the end of the chapter, we must *"stand fast and hold the traditions which you were taught, whether by word or our epistle"* (v.15), which is to say, hold fast to Apostolic

Tradition. When we hear a teaching, we must examine it against the truth of Scripture and Apostolic Traditions of the Church. We must keep Apostolic teaching and Holy Tradition pure.

2:3-12 Although it is not for us to know the day or season of the Second Coming of the Lord Christ, there are some prophecies about signs that will precede the Last Day of which we can be aware without actually pinpointing a particular date for the Second Coming.

2:3 Let no one deceive you by any means; for that Day will not come unless the falling away comes first. The first sign that St. Paul discusses as being a precursor to the day of rapture, Christ's Second Coming, and judgment, is *"falling away."* In essence, this simply refers to apostasy, at which time most Christians will, unfortunately, deny Christ and will turn their backs on the Church. This is what is called general apostasy or general falling away.

and the man of sin is revealed, the son of perdition. The second sign serving as a herald of the Second Coming is the Antichrist. Why did St. Paul call the Antichrist *"the man of sin"*? He will be the tool of Satan to spread and preach lawlessness and sin. He also called him the *"son of perdition." "Perdition"* refers to a state of eternal punishment or damnation. The Antichrist bears this title because the Lord will destroy Him and place Him in the lake of fire for his evil deeds.

2:4   who opposes. St. Paul describes the Antichrist as the one who will oppose Christ, the Church, the believers, the worshippers, the truth, and all Christ's teachings. When a person comes and begins to oppose all of those things, then this might be the Antichrist.

and exalts himself above all that is called God or that is worshiped, so that he sits as God. Why did St. Paul not instead say, *"exalts himself above God"*? That is because the Antichrist will not believe that he is above God, but will believe that he is God.

✤ *Heresies that prepare the path for the Antichrist* ~ Some heresies right now have started to pave the way for the coming of the Antichrist. I remember that recently another bishop and I were in Cairo and met with a Mormon. In Mormonism, they teach, in effect, that each person can eventually become an actual god. So we asked him, "Do you believe that you are god?" He answered, "I am god to my children." Then we asked him, "Are you god with a small 'g,' or God with a capital

'g'"? He replied, "capital 'G.' Here is, therefore, an example of some who hold beliefs which pave the way for the Antichrist who will exalt himself above all that is called God and will sit as God in the temple of God.

in the temple of God. To which temple does this refer? The Church Fathers are split into two groups in interpreting this part of the verse. Is this the Temple of Solomosolon? Will the Antichrist rebuild the Temple of Solomon and enter into it and literally sit in it as God? Or does this refer to the Church of the New Testament? Some of the Church Fathers say that this temple is *"of God,"* which in the New Testament era in which St. Paul wrote and preached, must refer to a legitimate house of God, which in Christianity is the Church rather than the Old Testament temple. This notion is furthered by the belief that God spoke of the Old Testament temple saying, *"Your house is left to you desolate"* (Matt. 23:38). This verse is interpreted as meaning that the Lord Jesus Christ was speaking of the desolate state of the Temple of Solomon, which they would not be able to rebuild again (and which after 2000 years still is the case). Thus, while some Church Fathers deemed the temple to refer to the Temple of Solomon, others considered it to refer to the New Testament Christian Church. ✤ Alternatively, we can think of this in a spiritual way. The temple of God is our hearts: *"Do you not know that you are the temple of God and that the*

Spirit of God dwells in you?" (1 Cor. 3:16). Therefore, for the Christians that believe in the Antichrist, it is as if they are allowing him to sit in their hearts. In this way, the Antichrist can be regarded as sitting as God in the temple of God.

showing himself that he is God. As St. Paul explains later, the Antichrist will perform many *"signs, and lying wonders"* (v.9) in order to deceive people so that people will believe that he is God.

2:5   Do you not remember that when I was still with you I told you these things? Apparently, when St. Paul preached in the city of Thessalonica, he taught them about the Second Coming of Christ and also about the Antichrist. This shows us that it is very important to learn and be reminded all the time about the signs of the Second Coming of the Lord so that we can discern between true and false teachers. ❖ It is our responsibility as parents and servants to teach our children about the Antichrist so that they are not easily deceived. Although the Antichrist is a man, the spirit of the Antichrist is working in this chapter, as St. Paul explains in this chapter. The spirit of *"lawlessness is already at work"* (v.7), and we must warn our children lest they be deceived and *"they should believe the lie"* and *"be condemned"* (v.11-12). Mormonism is an example of a teaching is line with

this spirit of lawlessness. Mormon teaching that people will become gods is a heresy and we must stand strongly against it to protect our children from such impure teaching.

2:6   And now you know what is restraining, that he may be revealed in his own time. There is something restraining the Antichrist from being revealed, in order that he appears in his own time. Thus, *"what is restraining"* is a power appointed by God to restrain the man of sin from appearing until he will be revealed. When the plan of salvation was started by the Lord from the time of His crucifixion, Satan likewise put a plan in place for the destruction of the world and its deception. There is a war between Satan and God. In the plan of Satan, the Antichrist is to appear and deceive the people. According to this plan, Satan seeks to prevail over God. Satan wants to make this Antichrist appear, but God is restraining him until the number of the elect is fulfilled. That is why God is restraining Satan and the appearance of the Antichrist. ❖ God has control over the times and seasons, and as He appeared in the *"fullness of time"* (Gal. 4:4), we are to understand that every event's timing is within the authority of God. Satan cannot and will not be able to change the times and seasons which the Father has put in His own authority. When his time comes, the power of God, which is restraining the

Antichrist, will be taken out of the way and the man of sin—the lawless one will be revealed. ❖ Many people interpret the phrase *"what is restraining"* in different ways. Some believe that this refers to the Church by the way of the Holy Spirit. Let us read the verses that follow to understand whether such an interpretation is legitimate.

2:7 For the mystery of lawlessness is already at work. Although the man of sin has not been revealed yet, "the mystery of lawlessness is already at work." It is working, but in a hidden way, until the man of sin will come. You may ask yourself, "All the sins I see around me, and yet you say it is hidden?" Yes, in comparison to the general apostasy and the time of the appearance of the man of sin, things are hidden, considered like a mystery that is not apparent to everyone. Generally, today we can say we are Christian and preach, but during the time of the revelation of the man of sin, he will oppose anyone mentioning the name of Christ. The spirit of lawlessness will at that time truly be in control. Until now, we call it sin and lawlessness, but at that time, it will be regarded as the norm. ❖ The way is being paved for the normalcy of such lawlessness. For example, homosexuality is becoming acceptable as being normal more and more. People give sin different names to take it out of mind as being a sin. Abortion is not called murder, but "pro-

choice." These are examples of how the mystery of lawlessness is at work, yet even now, there are those who oppose such lawlessness. Yet, at the time of the Antichrist, it will not be as such. Sin will be the norm, and there will be a great *"falling away"* (v.3).

only He who now restrains will do so until he is taken out of the way. Only God, who now restrains the Antichrist by His power, will postpone the appearance of the Antichrist, until that power is taken out of the way.
❖ Protestant teaching, reflected in this verse by capitalizing the second "he," is that the Holy Spirit is the one who is restraining the Antichrist. If we were to read this according to their teaching, the verse would read, "Only God, who now restrains, will do so until the Holy Spirit is taken out of the way." This teaching is very old, actually, from the time of St. John Chrysostom. St. John Chrysostom refuted this teaching saying that this power cannot be the Holy Spirit. Rather, when the time of the Antichrist comes, God will take away the power that restrains the Antichrist.
❖ This power cannot refer to the Holy Spirit because God promised us that the Holy Spirit will remain with us until the very end.
❖ Another opinion is that this power is the Church of the gentiles, and that they will be taken away (that is rapture) before the time of the Antichrist and the great tribulation. This alternative interpretation cannot withstand the other verses in the Bible that make clear

that rapture is to happen at the time of the Second Coming, and not before the great tribulation as many Protestant churches teach.

✠ We do not know what this power is that is restraining the Antichrist. What we know is that this power is from the Lord. Maybe the power of Christ binding Satan after His crucifixion is the power spoken of in this verse (cf., Ps. 72:9, Matt. 12:29, Is. 53:10, Luke 10:17, Acts 2:34-36, Col 2:15, Eph 4:8, Rev 20:1-6). After taking away this power, Satan will be able to reveal the man of sin and son of perdition.

✠ It is enough for us to understand that there is a power that God is using to restrain the man of sin—which power, God will take out of the way at the appointed time.

2:8 And then the lawless one will be revealed. Here, St. Paul calls him the lawless one because he will spread the *"mystery of lawlessness"* (v.7), at which time people will not abide with the law of God but rather by their own laws (see also commentary on v.7).

whom the Lord will consume with the breath of His mouth and destroy with the brightness of His coming. After St. Paul spoke about the apostasy and the appearance of the lawless one who will oppose every power and Christ Himself showing himself to be as God, he wants to encourage us by expressing the weakness of the

lawless one who will be consumed by the breath of the Lord's mouth. This imagery makes us think of blowing out a candle, which takes little effort to extinguish the insignificant flame. The message here is, "If you are with God, do not be afraid." St. Paul further describes the Lord's victory of the Antichrist by saying that when the Lord comes on the clouds (cf., 1 Th. 4:17, Mark 14:62) with the brightness of His glory, the lawless one and Satan will be destroyed. We should, therefore, abide in the Lord and stand fast in Him. We must not be afraid. Satan and this man can do nothing in the face of God.

2:9 The coming of the lawless one is according to the working of Satan, with all power, signs, and lying wonders. Satan is making a plan to overcome God. Part of his plan is to bring this person into the who will say he is the messiah. This will be *"according to the working of Satan,"* who will give the Antichrist power, signs, and wonders. Do you remember the story of Moses who worked a miracle in front of Pharaoh? Pharaoh brought his own magicians who were able to mimic the same sign, turning their rod into a serpent (Ex. 7:8-13; recall that the serpent from Moses' rod swallowed up the others). Miracles can, therefore, be done by the power of God or by the power of Satan. The Antichrist will come with the power of

Satan performing miracles. ❖ From this, therefore, we can understand the need to be very careful in our discernment of bona fide miracles. Many people immediately presume that miracles are always from God. That is not right, as St. John tells us, *"Beloved, do not believe every spirit, but test the spirits, whether they are of God; because many false prophets have gone out into the world"* (1 John 4:1; *"Test all things; hold fast what is good."*—1 Th. 5:21). We must examine miracles and determine whether they are from God. Those who do not do so, running after every miracle and sin, will be deceived when the Antichrist comes.

❖ *What about the miracles on television?* ~ Many people ask us about the miracles that they see on television. Examine such miracles and do not believe every miracle. It is not simply because some supernatural event occurs that it is necessarily from God. Satan will give the Antichrist such power.

2:10 and with all unrighteous deception. The Antichrist will come with all *"unrighteous deception,"* deceiving many people, convincing them that unrighteousness is the right way. This is the power of Satan, which lies in his ability to deceive. If he lost this power to deceive, he would be powerless. The Antichrist will cause people to consider unrighteousness as the norm. (And as I explained in

verse 7 above), see how homosexuality, abortion, and pre-marital sex have become widely acceptable, given a different name as a cloak for the true sins that they are. Think of the tolerance of heresies and the acceptance of unprofitable religions that blaspheme against God and in turn are intolerant of the truth. We have to have a strong stand to teach our children that the mystery of lawlessness (v.7) is at work right now and that they must discern the truth.

among those who perish, because they did not receive the love of the truth, that they might be saved. What is the field of the Antichrist's ministry? Who will believe him? Those who *"did not receive the love of the truth,"* and because they followed the *"son of perdition"* (v.3), they will likewise share in his demise and also *"perish."*

receive the love of the truth. We have a responsibility to teach our children the love of the truth. They have to receive it from us. Not only that they receive the truth, but how to love it. Many times when we teach the truth, people become rebellious to the truth. However, since *"the truth shall make you free"* (John 8:32)—the truth being God—we must teach the love of the truth. It is dire that servants and parents teach children this. Unfortunately, many parents say, "No, I will not teach my children such devotion because they will be prejudicial in their outlook.

Instead, I will teach them, 'Everything is before you, determine your own belief system.'" Sadly, if that is what we are doing, then our children will not receive the love of the truth. Love of the truth leads to salvation (*"that they might be saved"*), while rejecting the love of truth leads to perishing and destruction.   .

2:11   And for this reason God will send them strong delusion, that they should believe the lie. St. Paul says here something that may be difficult for many to understand at first. *"For this reason (i.e., because certain people will not love the truth) God will send the strong delusion."* Why would God do that? It is not meant to deceive them, because they have already chosen to love falsehood. God will, however, send them strong delusion in order to expose them. Many people may feel sympathetic to those who do not love the truth, even conjuring up defenses on their behalf. (Think of the example of homosexuality or abortion, for example, which people today teach is something natural or permissible). God will, therefore, send them strong delusion to expose them so that we can differentiate between the children of God and the children of the devil, as St. John tells us: *"In this the children of God and the children of the devil are manifest: Whoever does not practice righteousness is not of God, nor is he who does not love his brother."*

that they should believe the lie. St. Paul says "the lie," not "the lies." He is referring to the Antichrist, who believing in him, they will perish with him. For help in understanding this passage, we can turn to Ezekiel 14:4-5 where in essence, we read the same message. *"Therefore speak to them, and say to them, "Thus says the Lord GOD: 'Everyone of the house of Israel who sets up his idols in his heart, and puts before him what causes him to stumble into iniquity, and then comes to the prophet, I the LORD will answer him who comes, according to the multitude of his idols, that I may seize the house of Israel by their heart, because they are all estranged from Me by their idols."'* Here, the Lord is saying, if someone puts *"idols in his heart"* instead of God, then when he goes to the prophet to ask him about the will of God, He will answer them according to their idols. Why would God do that? Because they have already chosen their idols over God: *"because they are all estranged from Me by their idols."* This is the message which St. Paul is relaying here.

2:12   that they all may be condemned who did not believe the truth but had pleasure in unrighteousness. The exposure of those who do not love the truth (v.11) is very important to see the righteousness and justice of God. It will be clear to everyone that they will be condemned because they *"did not believe the truth"* and *"had pleasure in unrighteousness."* It is so sad to see how in today's times the extent to which people take *"pleasure in unrighteousness,"* accepting such sins as homosexuality and pre-marital sex with joyful affirmation. Unfortunately, people who believe in God are very weak when they are confronted with such things, often reverting to the common remark, *"I do not judge, I do not speak about such things, I respect their opinion."* What do you respect? You respect unrighteousness and lawlessness? There is no doubt we love sinners, but we do not respect unrighteousness and lawlessness.

2:13-17 Have expounded at length on the Antichrist, St. Paul concludes this chapter with a brighter message encouraging the Thessalonians to stand fast in their faith and hold strongly to Holy Tradition.

2:13 **But we are bound to give thanks to God always for you.** Looking at the punishment of sinners and the penalty that awaits lawless people makes the heart of the apostle feel "bound to give thanks to God" for the righteous who are always striving to abide in truth. When St. Paul remembers the Thessalonians, who were shedding their blood for the truth, he felt *"bound to give thanks to God."*

brethren beloved by the Lord, because God from the beginning chose you for salvation through sanctification by the Spirit and belief in the truth. The willingness of the Thessalonians to strive even to bloodshed because of their love of the truth comes by the grace of God, without whom nothing is possible (*"With men it is impossible, but with God all things are possible."*—Matt. 19:26). That is why he tells them that he is grateful for the strength of their faith, knowing that it is by God that this is so. ❖ Notice in this verse, we see our relationship with the Holy Trinity and salvation in the following four points:

beloved by the Lord. (1) of 4. The Son of God loved us, shedding his blood for us (*"God demonstrates His own love toward us, in that while we were still sinners, Christ died for us."*—Rom. 5:8).

because God from the beginning chose you for salvation. (2) of 4. God the Father chose everyone for salvation, but not everyone accepted His salvation.

through sanctification by the Spirit. (3) of 4. The third hypostasis of the Holy Trinity, the Holy Spirit, sanctifies us through the Sacraments of the Church to be saved.

and belief in the truth. (4) of 4. The human role in the plan of salvation is belief in the truth. The Lord loved us and died for us. The Father chose us all for salvation. The Holy Spirit sanctifies us to receive it. But, salvation is finally effectuated by our accepting it.

2:14 **to which He called you.** As spoken about in the previous verse, the Holy Trinity worked out our salvation, which we can receive if we accept it. In order for people to respond to the plan of salvation, they must be taught about it, wherein lies the role which evangelism has in Christianity. God called people to the knowledge of the truth by the preaching of the apostles. Here we understand the importance of evangelism and sharing the truth with others. Go and share the saving truth with others, because God called everyone to the knowledge of the truth. We are His tools and instruments to share the knowledge of the true God.

by our gospel. St. Paul does not mean, "the Gospel of St. Paul," but rather the preaching of the apostles. Here, St. Paul can be said to refer to Holy Tradition.

for the obtaining of the glory of our Lord Jesus Christ. What is the ultimate goal of salvation? What does salvation mean? It means you will be glorified with Christ in the kingdom of heaven. You will obtain glory with God, as Christ prayed: *"And the glory which You gave Me I have given them, that they may be one just as We are one"* (John 17:22).

2:15 **Therefore, brethren, stand fast and hold the traditions which you were taught.** We must stand fast to our faith and hold on tightly to Holy Tradition, and when someone comes to us with something contrary, we must not accept it. St. Paul said elsewhere, *"But even if we, or an angel from heaven, preach any other gospel to you than what we have preached to you, let him be accursed"* (Gal. 1:8). Satan is trying to deceive believers. How do we protect ourselves from deception? We must *"stand fast and hold the traditions which you were taught."*

traditions ... whether by word or our epistle. St. Paul spoke here about two different kinds of tradition: oral (*"by word"*), or written (*"epistle"*). The Holy Scripture is part of written tradition, but then, there is also oral tradition. I am saying this because Protestants profess belief solely in the Bible: "If it is in the Bible, I believe. Otherwise I will not." They do not comprehend that oral tradition is more ancient than the Scripture (written tradition). Think of the following example. We say now that the Bibles we have in our hands are canonical (i.e., included in the list of official Christian writings accepted as genuine). There are other books that are considered not canonical. Who told you that the Gospel according to St. Matthew is canonical, and the gospel of Barnabas is not? Is there a verse in the Bible telling you the answer to this question? No, but rather oral tradition is from where the answer comes. How can we attack Holy Tradition then? It is oral tradition that gave us the Holy Scriptures. Those who attack Holy Tradition are likewise essentially attacking the basis for their belief in the Bible. Holy Tradition is considered to include Holy Scripture, the teachings of the apostles, the early church fathers (including liturgical books as a product of the fathers), and the ecumenical councils. If anyone attacks tradition, now you know to which verse to point in response.

are received without addition or deletion.

- Against Heresies (4, 33, 8)

✠ St. Epiphanius of Salamis ✠

(c. AD 374–378)

It is needful also to make use of Tradition; for not everything can be gotten from Sacred Scripture. The holy apostles handed down some things in the Scriptures, other things in Tradition.

- Against All Heresies (61, 6)

~ In their own words: what the early Christians thought of oral tradition. ~

✠ St. Irenaeus ✠

(c. AD 180–199)

The true gnosis [i.e., knowledge of spiritual mysteries] is the doctrine of the Apostles, and the ancient organization of the Church throughout the whole world, and the manifestation of the body of Christ according to the succession of bishops, by which successions of the bishops have handed down the Church which is found everywhere; and the very complete tradition of the Scriptures, which have come down to us by being guarded against falsification, and which

✠ St. Jerome ✠

(c. AD 379 or 382)

[Speaking about baptism and the invocation of the Holy Spirit as being] The custom of the Churches… Do you demand to know where it is written?.... Even if it had not the authority of Scripture the consent of the whole world in this matter would confer on it the force of precept. For there are many other observances in the Church which, though due to Tradition, have acquired the authority of the written law, as for instance the practicing of dipping the head three times in the baptismal font … and there are many other unwritten practices the observance of which is vindicated by reason.

- Dialogue Between a Luciferian and an Orthodox Christian (8).

☩ Scholar Tertullian ☩

(c. AD 200)

Wherever it shall be clear that the truth of the Christian discipline and faith are present, there also will be found the truth of the Scriptures and of their explanation, and of all the Christian traditions.

- Demurrer Against the Heretics (19, 3)

☩ St. Basil the Great ☩

(c. AD 375)

Of the dogmas and kerygmas [i.e., preaching or proclamations] preserved in the Church, some we possess from written teaching and others we receive from the tradition of the Apostles, handed on to us in a mystery. In respect to piety both are of the same force. No one will contradict any of those, no one, at any rate, who is even moderately versed in matters ecclesiastical. Indeed, were we to try to reject unwritten

customs as having no great authority, we would unwittingly injure the Gospel in its vitals …

For instance, to take the first and most general example, who taught us in writing to sign with the sign of the cross those who have trusted in the name of our Lord Jesus Christ? What writing has taught us to turn to the East in prayer? Which of the saints left us in writing the words of the epiclesis at the consecration of the Bread of Eucharist and the Cup of Benediction? For we are not content with those words the Apostle or the gospel has recorded, but we say other things also, both before and after; and we regard those other words, which we received from unwritten teaching, as being of great importance to the mystery.

Where is it written that we are to bless the baptismal water, the oil of anointing, and even the one who is being baptized? Is it not from silent and mystical tradition? Indeed, in what written word is even the anointing with oil taught? Where does it say that in baptizing there is to be a triple immersion? And the rest of the things done at Baptism—where is it written that we are to renounce Satan and his angels? Does this not come from the secret and arcane teaching which our

Fathers guarded in a silence not too curiously meddled with and not idly investigated, when they had learned well that reverence for the mysteries is best preserved by silence....

In the same way the Apostles and Fathers who, in the beginning, prescribed the Church's rites, guarded in secrecy and silence the dignity of the mysteries; for that which is handing on of unwritten precepts and practices: that the knowledge of our dogmas may not be neglected and held in contempt by the multitude through too great a familiarity. Dogma and kerygma are two distinct things. Dogma is observed in silence.

- The Holy Spirit (27, 66)

comfort and hope in eternal life to be strengthened and encouraged. St. Paul reminds them that God did not leave us alone, but rather gave us *"everlasting consolation"* (beyond the time of this life) by His grace.

2:17 comfort your hearts and establish you in every good word and work. St. Paul speaks about their feelings, works, and their behavior (their heart, mouth, and work). His prayer here is focused on the Thessalonians receiving emotional comfort, so that they can then adequately preach appropriately by word and their behavior will likewise be manifested to comport with that of true Christians.

2:16 Now may our Lord Jesus Christ Himself, and our God and Father, who has loved us and given us everlasting consolation and good hope by grace. St. Paul ends the chapter with a prayer to God the Father and the Lord Jesus Christ. God loves us, and by His grace, we have hope and everlasting consolation. Recall that the Thessalonian Christians suffered persecution and needed

Chapter 2 Questions

1. What are the two signs that will occur before the second coming of the Lord?

2. What are the features of the man of sin?

3. What did St. Paul mean by "what is restraining"?

4. Who will believe him?

5. Why will God send them strong delusion?

6. What are the elements of salvation?

7. What is Holy Tradition?

3

Chapter Outline

- Request for prayers (1-5)
- Warning against idleness (6-15)
- Benediction (16-18)

of zeal for others who have not heard the word of God. As you have heard the word of God which is glorified by your lives, you also should labor so that the word of God may reach others and be glorified in their lives as well. We cannot remain content with the fact that we go to church and behave in a Christian manner, but we have the responsibility spread the word of God to others.

3:1 Finally, brethren, pray for us. St. Paul is asking for prayer, and this shows his humility. Those who have spiritual responsibilities need more prayers than anyone else. That is why we pray for our patriarch, the bishops, and the priests.

that the word of the Lord may run swiftly. The hope is that the word of the Lord spreads quickly with no obstacles or hindrances. This is the true heart of a servant and a shepherd, seeking that the word of God spreads all over the world. That is why he was asking them to pray for the swift spreading of the word of God.

and be glorified. St. Paul is seeking that people are transformed by the word of God, changing their lives because of it. When we accept the word of God, live by it, and are transformed by it, the word of God is glorified in our lives.

just as it is with you. Do not be content that you know Christ and the word of God. Your heart should be full

3:2 and that we may be delivered from unreasonable and wicked men. St. Paul here indicates another reason why he seeks the prayers of the Thessalonians. Do not think that he seeks personal deliverance, for he writes elsewhere, *"For to me, to live is Christ, and to die is gain"* (Phil. 1:21). St. Paul was seeking that unreasonable and wicked people do not hinder him from preaching the word of God and sharing the good news of salvation.

unreasonable. This refers to people who argue without foundation, just wasting time and distracting people. Instead of energy being directed to sharing the word of God, unreasonable people argue with people, causing preachers to waste their energy in unfruitful discussions.

wicked men. This refers to those who persecute ministers and preachers to stop them from preaching the word of

God.

for not all have faith. This is the reality of life. This life is full of people who are unreasonable and who are wicked, who seek that the preaching of the word of God to cease, opposing Christians. We deal with this reality by prayer. ✤ Praying regarding such situations is the responsibility of all of us. When the deacon says in the Divine Liturgy, "Pray for the Holy Gospel," we need to lift our hearts and pray "that the word of the Lord may run swiftly," be "glorified," and that unreasonable and wicked men will not disturb or cause a hindrance to the spreading and preaching of the word of God.

3:3 But the Lord is faithful, who will establish you and guard you from the evil one. We deal with the reality of wicked and unreasonable people by prayer. We do not trust in ourselves, but in the faithfulness of God. Unreasonable and wicked men are the tools of *"the evil one."* Satan uses them, but the faithful Lord can overcome Satan.

establish ... guard. St. Paul seeks the Lord to establish the Thessalonians so they are not shaken in their faith because of the severity of persecution, and also to protect them (*"guard"*) from the evil one. God will establish and guard us, not because of our righteousness

and goodness, but because of His faithfulness.

3:4 And we have confidence in the Lord concerning you, both that you do and will do the things we command you. This is a very good example of the relationship between the pastor and his flock. This relationship is based on confidence that his commands and instructions to them will be taken seriously and will be followed, being done now and also in the future. And this is expected of the flock not only in pastor's presence, but also in his absence, because this is true obedience. If anyone is considering not obeying, then by setting up the expectation that he has confidence that they "do and will do" the things commanded of them, then the flock will live to these expectations, feeling encouraged by the confidence placed in the Lord concerning them. ✤ As parents, if you set the right expectations for your children, they will live up to those expectations. If, however, parents tell their children from the outset, "I know you will not obey me," or, "I know you will not listen to me," then their children will consider why they should even follow the commandments delivered by their parents.

confidence in the Lord. St. Paul exhibits tremendous confidence in the Lord, who will establish the Thessalonians, guard them, and direct their lives. Our hope is not in people, but rather it should be in God. That is why, when parents come to me complaining about their children, for example, and say they have lost hope that their children will change, I tell them to put their confidence in the Lord who can guard, establish, and direct them.

3:5   Now may the Lord direct your hearts into the love of God. It is God who helps us to grow in spiritual virtues. It is the Holy Spirit who directs us to grow in love and patience, which are the fruit of the Holy Spirit (Gal. 5:22). Love is needed to endure persecution (from which the Thessalonians were suffering). Their endurance of persecution was not out of helplessness or due to a feeling of oppression and despair, but rather their response to such suffering was to accept persecution because of their love for God. ❖ We need to grow in the love of God all the time, because God is love, and God is infinite, so love is also infinite. No one can claim they have reached perfection in the virtue of love. Thus, St. Paul prays for the Thessalonians that the Lord directs them to grow in the love of God, especially in the face of persecution.

.

3:5 and into the patience of Christ. After expressing a belief (in v.4 above) that the Thessalonians will readily obey his commands, St. Paul now gives one command. This command is directed to the whole church.

in the name of our Lord Jesus Christ. This has two meanings. First, St. Paul is speaking with authority. Second, the commandment he is about to pronounce is from God, and not simply from men.

that you withdraw from every brother who walks disorderly and not according to the tradition which he received from us. St. Paul is asking the Thessalonians (and us) to withdraw by not communicating or having communion with (and thus, in effect, akin to excommunication) every believer (*"brother"*) who does not walk in accordance with tradition. St. Paul differentiates between two types of traditions: Holy Tradition (Apostolic Tradition), and also the traditions of men. Many people want to add new things to the Church and insert their own traditions, often in disregard of Holy Tradition of the Church. St. Paul says, "No, this is not acceptable. If anyone walks disorderly, they must be excommunicated. Withdraw from him." That is because *"God is not the author of confusion but of peace, as in all the churches of the saints"* (1 Cor. 14:33). Can you imagine if everyone started to enforce their own beliefs and regulations within the Church? We would lose our unity and uniformity of Churches.

disorderly. This word (which in Greek is "ἀτάκτως"; "a" [signifying a lack of] "taktous" [meaning order]; this word is similar to the Arabic word used to refer to the rites of the Church, which is "tukous" or "tuks" [طقوس]). There is a certain rite and ritual and it is not up to just any person to change them. Why does St. Paul say this?   See the next verse.

3:7   **For you yourselves know how you ought to follow us, for we were not disorderly among you.** Holy Tradition was handed to us either through the writings that we received in the Holy Scriptures and through some other trusted means: for example, the Letters, Gospel accounts, Book of Revelation, and the Book of Acts, or through the canons of the Apostles, or through the writings of their disciples (the Apostolic or Early Church Fathers) or through Ecumenical Councils. Tradition can be either oral or written. It is very clear that since the beginning of the Church, it followed certain rites and/or rituals.   We can conclude that during the forty days just before the Ascension of our Lord Jesus Christ, He discussed with the apostles some rites and rituals, and these rituals were passed down to us from the Apostles who themselves followed these rites, as St. Paul told them, *"for you yourselves*

know how you ought to follow us, for we were not disorderly among you."

3:8-10   nor did we eat anyone's bread free of charge, but worked with labor and toil night and day, that we might not be a burden to any of you, not because we do not have authority, but to make ourselves an example of how you should follow us.   For even when we were with you, we commanded you this: If anyone will not work, neither shall he eat. Although St. Paul, as an apostle, has the authority to eat from the altar—because the Lord made a rule that the servant of the altar should eat from the altar (1 Cor. 9:14; also see Heb 13:10 and Numbers 18:21)—yet, in light of the new budding Churches who were suffering persecution, St. Paul did not take advantage of his authority. Besides preaching, he was working day and night in order to support his needs and the needs of those for whom he preached.   He also did this in order to set an example for them that, *"If anyone will not work, neither shall he eat."*   While the Lord entitled those who preach the gospel to live from the gospel, and although it is incumbent upon the believers to support them, St. Paul, nonetheless, did not want to overburden the Thessalonians and wanted to set an example for them. Thus, the crux of the message is this: "If we are entitled to be sustained by you, yet, we do not take advantage of that, then how come some of you refuse to work and impose a burden on others to support you? This is not acceptable." St. Paul reminded them clearly that, *"if anyone will not work, neither shall he eat."*

that we might not be a burden to any of you. This is a lesson for all of us regarding the notion that we should not be a burden to anyone. We should not make ourselves comfortable at the expense of others. For example, nowadays, in many families, both husbands and wives work. However, is it right when a husband returns home for him to demand from his wife to do everything for him without helping her? That is not acceptable. Do not be a burden on others. She is working like you are working. Be sensitive to others, and as much as you can, do not burden others with your needs. If you can serve your own needs, this will be very helpful.

If anyone will not work, neither shall he eat. Here in the Church, if someone comes to us and needs support, and the Church finds the person a job, yet, he refuses to work and seeks continued support, then based on the instructions of St. Paul in this chapter, the Church should not provide for that person. Otherwise, the Church would be encouraging bad behavior and laziness. Instead of helping people with money, we need to help them with finding work and labor, so that they can provide for their own needs. As they say, if someone asks for a fish, give him a net with which he can catch for himself many fish.

3:11 **For we hear that there are some who walk among you in a disorderly manner, not working at all, but are busybodies.** St. Paul considered it to be "disorder" when a person does not follow the regulation and arrangement that those who do not work shall not eat.

3:12 **Now those who are such we command and exhort through our Lord Jesus Christ.** Through the authority given to the apostles by the Lord Jesus Christ, St. Paul commanded (like giving an apostolic order) and exhorted (signifying "teaching") that the rule announced in the previous verses should be followed for their own benefit. We need to learn how to be responsible, and as parents, we need to teach our children to be responsible, to take care of themselves and participate in various things around the house. Responsibility is taught from childhood.

that they work in quietness and eat their own bread. Work without complaining. Be grateful that you have a job. Many people wish they could work but do not have an opportunity to do so. Be thankful and work in quietness. ✠ St. Paul here is following the teaching of God, who was able to cover all the needs of Adam and Eve with plenty to sustain more than just the two persons who were created. Nonetheless, the Lord asked Adam to work in the land and toil because God wants His children to be responsible, although it would have been very easy for Adam and Eve's needs to be satisfied by God alone. The Lord Jesus Christ Himself, when He was a child, helped Joseph the Carpenter and worked with him.

3:13 **But as for you, brethren, do not grow weary in doing good.** Many times when we start to do good, labor and toil, we get very tired. St. Paul teaches on the contrary not to feel too weary with the duties of life. Instead, we should continue doing good which will be helpful in spiritual maturity and growth. Although Satan will exhaust you, the grace of God is there to help us overcome and not to *"grow weary in doing good."* Do not choose what is simply convenient and easy, but choose what is right.

3:14 **And if anyone does not obey our word in this epistle, note that person and do not keep company with him, that he may be ashamed.** Apparently while St. Paul was in Thessalonica, he gave particular commands. Some people did not listen, and thus, that is why there is the need to have consequences for disobedience. Do not think that discipline is contradictory to love. Actually, as the Bible teaches us, *"whom the Lord loves He chastens"* (Heb. 12:6; *"You should know in your heart that as a man chastens his son, so the LORD your God chastens you."*—Deut. 8:5). If you love your son, you will discipline him. That is why St. Paul, out of love, sets forth a disciplinary action in case of disobedience. The purpose of such discipline is to lead the person to repentance. When such a person feels *"ashamed"* he will hopefully turn back.

3:15 **Yet do not count him as an enemy, but admonish him as a brother.** When proceeding with disciplinary action, do it with love. Do not consider it as if you are fighting an enemy, but rather admonishing and disciplining a beloved fellow Christian in order that the person will return back as a responsible member in the body of Christ. We should not treat mistakes as if the person making them has now turned into an enemy. This is not the right attitude.

✠ *Three features of disciplining* ~ As distilled from verses 14 and 15 above, (1) discipline does not contradict the notion of love, (2) the purpose of discipline is to bring the person to repentance, (3) we should exhort and admonish, teaching the person, and (4) this should be done with a spirit of love.

3:16 Now may the Lord of peace Himself give you peace always in every way. The Lord be with you all. As I mentioned previously, the Thessalonians were suffering from tremendous persecution. During such times of suffering, people often lose their peace. St. Paul is therefore reminding them that the God whom we worship and abides in our hearts is the *"Lord of peace."* He is the prince of peace and its author. May God, therefore, give us peace in every way.

3:17 The salutation of Paul with my own hand, which is a sign in every epistle; so I write. Remember earlier in this epistle, St. Paul told the Thessalonians *"not to be soon shaken in mind or troubled, either by spirit or by word or by letter, as if from us"* (2 Thess. 2:2). Apparently, many people tried to tell them that something was the teaching of St. Paul or fabricated letters as if from St. Paul, when in fact those teachings or letters were not derived from him. Thus, St. Paul here indicates how to verify the authenticity of his letters to them. St. Paul was, therefore, warning them to be sure that they are not receiving as authentic letters from him, those which were not. ✢ St. Paul

had a malady affecting his eyes, which caused him to have others write epistles for him, which he dictated to them. St. Paul would usually at least sign every letter once completed to authenticate it as being from him.

3:18 The grace of our Lord Jesus Christ be with you all. Amen. The difference between the Old and New Covenant is this one word: *"grace."* *"For the law was given through Moses, but grace and truth came through Jesus Christ"* (John 1:17).

~~~~~~~~~~

Chapter 3 Questions

1. For what two things does St. Paul ask them to pray on his behalf?

2. What confidence did St. Paul have in the Thessalonians?

3. What did St. Paul ask the Lord to do for the Thessalonians?

4. What had St. Paul commanded them, even when he was with them?

5. What did St. Paul command such busybodies to do?

6. What did St. Paul charge them to do if anyone did not obey his word in this epistle?

~~~~~~~~~~

www.ingramcontent.com/pod-product-compliance
Lightning Source LLC
LaVergne TN
LVHW061327060426
835511LV00012B/1902